C000260787

THE AUSTRALIAN HOUSE

A traditional timber house in a rural setting, relatively bare of decorative elements.

THE AUSTRALIAN HOUSE

Homes of the Tropical North

Balwant Saini, text   Ray Joyce, photography

LANSDOWNE

Distributed by Gary Allen Pty Ltd
9 Cooper Street, Smithfield, NSW 2164

Published by Lansdowne Publishing Pty Ltd
Level 5, 70 George Street, Sydney NSW 2000, Australia

First published by Lansdowne Press Pty Ltd 1982
Reprinted 1983, 1984, 1985, 1986, 1988,
Reprinted by Weldon Publishing 1990
Reprinted by Lansdowne Publishing Pty Ltd 1993, 1994

© Copyright: Lansdowne Publishing Pty Ltd 1982
© Copyright design: Lansdowne Publishing Pty Ltd 1982

Editor Diane Furness
Designed by Elaine Rushbrooke
Typeset in Australia by SA Typecentre, Adelaide
Printed in Hong Kong by Everbest Printing Co. Ltd

National Library of Australia Cataloguing-in-Publication Data

Saini, Balwant Singh, 1930– .
    The Australian house: homes of the tropical north.

    Includes index.
    ISBN 1 86302 098 5.

    1. Architecture, Domestic — Tropics. 2. Architecture, Tropical —
    Australia, Northern. 3. Building, Wooden — Tropics. 4. Building,
    Wooden —Australia, Northern. I. Joyce, Ray, 1947– . II. Title.

    728.370994290913

All rights reserved. Subject to the Copyright Act 1968, no part of this
publication may be reproduced, stored in a retrieval system, or transmitted,
in any form, or by any means, electronic, mechanical, photocopying,
recording or otherwise, without the prior written permission of the publisher.

CONTENTS

ACKNOWLEDGEMENTS

Many people have assisted us in the preparation of this book. We thank them all and especially architect, Ian Clayton, who helped collate much of the background material for the final chapter, 'Restoration and Renovation'.

Our special thanks to the National Trust of Queensland for permission to reproduce sketches and information from its publication *Ipswich: A Townscape Study*, and in particular to its Manager, Jim Fuller, and secretaries Helen Harris, Dorothy Gibson-Wilde and Maria Magoffin of Rockhampton, Townsville and Charters Towers, respectively, all of whom greatly facilitated our field visits.

To historian, Peter Bell, of James Cook University we extend thanks for his initial guidance and architects, Don Roderick, Richard Allom, and Bruce Buchanan for their valuable help and comments.

We would also like to acknowledge our indebtedness to Elaine Rushbrooke for the concept and her design and layout, and Janette Massey and Sonia Wilson for typing the original manuscript of the book.

And last, but not least, our sincere thanks go to all those who generously allowed us to interview them and to photograph their homes, often without adequate prior warning. For reasons of privacy and in order to repect their wish to remain anonymous, we have refrained from listing names and addresses. It is hardly necessary to emphasise that without their willing co-operation this book would not have been possible.

Balwant Saini
Ray Joyce

FOREWORD

To most Australians a tropical house conjures a vision of a large sprawling structure on round timber stumps with an extensive deep, shaded verandah filled with trellis and a blaze of colour spread by a bougainvillaea creeper, with a tall mango tree or two shading its red corrugated iron roof.

There is an open friendliness about these houses which, like their owners, is characteristic of the warmer regions of Australia which comprise well over seventy per cent of this vast continent. They reflect a lifestyle which is a unique expression of the way people have adapted themselves to an environment vastly different from their historic European experience. These qualities have also given these houses a peculiarly Australian form of vernacular character not found elsewhere.

So it is all the more difficult to understand why architectural historians have largely tended to ignore this important form of Australia's cultural heritage. Those who have seen fit to discuss it, have usually only made a passing reference to it.

Lately there is an increasing interest in these houses which not only reflects the revived awareness of Australians in their own heritage but also stems from pragmatic reasons, since these houses offer what is increasingly becoming a scarce commodity — space. What's more, it can be obtained at a low cost by using materials which are light and simple and can be used in a structural system which is neither labour intensive nor time consuming.

Although many of these timber houses were built during the latter half of the nineteenth and early twentieth centuries, they seem to have survived remarkably well. In some inner city areas, a number of them are being demolished to make way for office buildings or blocks of units, but good examples can still be found in the older sections of the large cities and country towns of tropical Australia.

Many owners of these houses are not often aware of the importance and value of their buildings. Others, who are better informed and who are planning to restore, renovate or extend, do not always know which steps to take to ensure that the changes in design and construction preserve the authenticity of their style.

The aim of this book is to remedy this situation. It critically looks at the main features of these houses to assess to what extent they satisfy the demands of tropical living. In the Introduction, the origins of this unique house are discussed in the light of historical, geographic and economic factors which have influenced their development over the last 150 years. The major portion of this book is devoted to a detailed photographic study of the many components which have combined to create this unique Australian form of domestic architecture. Most of all, Ray Joyce's photographic study offers readers a glimpse of the extraordinary world of beauty and charm which is characteristic of these structures.

The concluding chapter, 'Restoration and Renovation', (of particular interest to owners and potential buyers) adds a final, practical, and down-to-earth note to a publication which is a celebration of a unique form of Australian architecture.

Balwant Saini
March 1981

INTRODUCTION

This remarkable form of domestic architecture can trace its origins to a number of sources. It has evolved primarly in the cities and towns of northern Australia and lends itself to a variety of building types; yet the ultimate climatic suitability of these houses remains a moot point.

Until recently, when discovery of enormous resources such as minerals and the growth of agricultural and tourist industries opened up considerable development, Australia's tropical regions have largely been ignored. Most of Australia's 15 million people have continued to live and work in a few urban centres located in the south-eastern coastal areas where the climate is cooler, rainfall is reliable and the soil is rich. The tropical regions (which constitute something like 75 per cent of the land) have largely supported very sparse populations, mainly in the form of scattered families associated with pastoral enterprises and a few single-industry towns such as mining and smaller commercial and administrative settlements whose livelihood depends upon the former.

Travelling through these settlements, one of the outstanding impressions one forms is that of a harsh landscape punctuated with little clusters of one or two storey timber and iron houses. They have a special vernacular charm which imparts to these settlements a distinctive character. They have vast spacious rooms with very high ceilings and ventilators and access from all four sides. The important rooms are surrounded by a deep

verandah, part of which is usually enclosed in order to accommodate cooking and washing facilities. The deep verandah and the secondary living rooms all around the main accommodation areas provide valuable shade and protect the walls from the heat of the direct tropical sun.

It is sad that in recent years many of these houses have been either demolished to make room for new buildings or altered and 'messed about with' to such a degree that they are hardly recognisable as good examples of early colonial architecture. Invariably the houses which replace them are very poor specimens of brick veneer villas more suited to the cooler climates of the southern cities.

An unfortunate result of all this is that many of Australia's tropical settlements are no longer unique and, if it were not for the lush vegetation which provides a marvellous backdrop to their hilly settings, they would be indistinguishable from any large sized suburbs of more temperate Melbourne or Sydney.

There is obviously an urgent need to create greater public awareness about the value of these houses so that, whenever possible, appropriate steps are taken to preserve this important segment of Australia's national heritage.

Testimony to the early and widespread use of timber and galvanised iron.

ORIGINS

Architectural historians who have traced the development of early domestic buildings in Australia have listed a number of primitive construction methods which have been widely used by the pioneers during the eighteenth and nineteenth centuries. They range from wattle-and-daub, earth, bark and rough timber slabs to more sound and durable structures of brick and stone. It is still possible to see some examples of these buildings in south-eastern Australia where early settlers were faced with prospects of constructing a basic shelter with little or no resources of durable materials and building labour.

The development of timber and iron ('tin') domestic structures of tropical regions followed at a comparatively later stage when these versatile and light-weight materials became extensively available in the country. Wattle-and-daub methods were never adopted because firstly there was no wattle in the semi-desert region and, secondly, in heavy rainfall areas it was difficult to apply clay as it was invariably washed away by heavy downpours.

One sees very few stone or even mud buildings in tropical Australia as they are essentially labour intensive. It is possible to see some isolated examples, such as the Telegraph Station in Alice Springs, but these were exceptions rather than the rule. The use of masonry was largely confined to important public buildings rather than domestic structures.

So it seems Australia's tropical houses are essentially light-weight timber and iron structures which are primarily the product of special local circumstances and the impact of scarcity of local materials and building skills. This is particularly the case in northern Australia, where according to historian, Peter Bell, of Townsville's James Cook University, large numbers of people were forced to build reasonably economic shelters in a hurry during the early agricultural and pastoral development and later mining boom over the second half of the nineteenth and early twentieth centuries. This enabled them to get on with their main task of extracting the maximum profits with the minimum delay. They were frontier people who had little time to build solid-permanent structures but grasped the opportunity to construct partially industrialised buildings

Before light-weight versatile materials such as timber and tin became available in tropical Australia, early pioneers had to rely on local resources. It is still possible to see a few examples of masonry structures in northern Australia such as this telegraph house in Alice Springs.

with light-weight materials (and these were mainly timber and iron which could be easily transported and which could be re-used in another structure at another location). In northern Australia, there are numerous examples where whole dwellings have been literally moved from one place to another, hundreds of kilometres away, and reassembled, incorporating alterations and additions to suit their new function.

This is partly why it is difficult to label definite sub-regional architectural styles. There are obvious minor features which are predominant in a specific area, such as the extension of the entrance verandah porch beyond the verandah line in Rockhampton, or the different forms of pediments over the entrances (which are semicircular in Toowoomba and triangular in Rockhampton). However, by and large, the basic structure and form of these houses is fairly similar and all house types can be found throughout the tropical region.

Another reason for the timber or tin 'temporary' character of these houses lay in the uncertainty of life which surrounded the early mining towns of north Queensland. Therefore, there was little incentive for people to put down permanent roots and build substantial and durable buildings.

Improved roads to inland areas made it possible to transport complete or partially assembled houses for accommodation in remote areas.

Contrary to geographical definition and judging from the point of view of climate and human comfort, tropical Australia includes all those uncomfortably hot areas where 30°C. temperatures are exceeded on more than 25 days in a year. They include both hot dry as well as hot humid regions and, together, add up to over 75 per cent of the land mass of the continent.

STRUCTURE

The basic structure of these houses is a fairly standardised timber frame made up of 50 x 100 millimetre studs mortised into top and bottom plates. They are lined, usually inside, with specially shaped timber slats locally known as chamferboards. These boards are nailed flush to the studs and diagonal braces are left exposed on the outside. This practice is not necessarily Australian as it is widely used in the English and American farm and other low-cost structures associated with outbuildings of major residential architecture.

Stud framing is essentially an extension of the earlier widely spaced uprights whose intervening spaces were filled up in a number of ways (including the use of straw-boards, mud, timber or brick walls). Hardwood studs of lighter sections, more closely spaced, are partly the product of sawmilling operations, which made it

possible to cut timber in more easily transportable sections and lengths. Much of present day carpentry practice in Australia uses this method and, incidentally, relies more heavily on industrialised products such as nails. The method demands less exacting skills, margin of error is less, and has therefore been readily accepted by semi-skilled builders throughout Australia.

In tropical Australia, earlier reliance on metal was soon replaced by a more extensive use of timber when this versatile building material began to arrive in large quantities from more developed population centres in the south. In coastal townships of the north, building materials already pre-cut and ready for use on site were shipped at less cost than transporting them overland over what was still a pretty rough country. A number of building material suppliers specialised in supplying complete kits for assembly in remote corners of northern Australia, thus establishing a tradition of prefabricated domestic building long before it was even heard of elsewhere in Australia.

The MITCHELL.

WIDE verandahs and a handsome exterior are features of The Mitchell. There are four bedrooms, and the dining-room and sitting-room, being connected with an arch, make an extremely large living-room. The detached kitchen is a feature greatly appreciated by those with experience of it. Note the specification.

SPECIFICATION:

Height of Studs, 11ft. 6in.
Plates and Bearers, 5 x 3 Hardwood.
Top Plates, 3 x 3 Hardwood.
Studs, 5 x 4, 3 x 3, and 3 x 2 Hardwood.
Floor Joists, 5 x 2 Hardwood.
Verandah Bottom Plates, 8 x 2 Hardwood.
Verandah Top Plate, 6 x 2½ Dressed Pine.
Ceiling Joists and Rafters, 4 x 2 Pine.
Verandah Posts and Newels, 4 x 4 Dressed Hardwood.
Flooring, 6½ x 1 T. & G. Pine and 4 x 1 Dressed Hardwood.
Sheeting to exposed Walls, 6½ x 1 Pine Chamfer Boards.
Sheeting to Walls under Verandah and Partitions, 4½ x 1 T. G. V. Pine.
Lining to exposed Walls and Ceilings, 4½ x ⅝ T. G. V. Pine.

Roof overhangs verandah 12 inches. Ceiling to all rooms. Scotia to ceilings. Fillets floors. Panel doors with fret panels over. Ledged doors to kitchen and verandah room. Fanlights over French lights, and front and back doors. Galvanised iron roofing, ridge capping, spouting, down-pipe, stove recess, and stump caps. Berger's B.P. Paints (prepared) and brushes for three coats externally. Locks, hinges, fittings, anchor bolts, nails, solder, etc. Materials for E.C. 5ft. x 4ft., walls 7ft.; framing fitted. Materials for 1,000-gallon tank and stand.

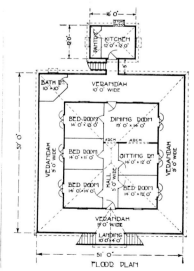

FLOOR PLAN

The DALBY.

THIS Home is quite different from most designs, as more than a third of the room space is occupied by a very large living room open to all breezes. French Lights let the breezes in and out. The Bedrooms are of good size and are always cool. The Kitchen is far enough away from the Living Room to exclude all noise and smell of cooking. If the roof of this home be coated with Arabic it will be as cool as any house could be. A study of the timbers used will show that the very best of everything is used throughout. This is an important consideration.

SPECIFICATION:

Height of Studs, 11ft. 6in.
Plates and Bearers, 5 x 3 Hardwood.
Top Plates, 3 x 3 Hardwood.
Studs, 5 x 4, 3 x 3, and 3 x 2 Hardwood.
Main Floor Joists, 5 x 2 Hardwood.
Verandah Floor Joists, 4 x 2 Hardwood.
Verandah Bottom Plates, 8 x 2 Hardwood.
Verandah Posts and Newels, 4 x 4 Dressed Hardwood.
Verandah Top Plates, 6 x 2½ Dressed Pine.
Ceiling Joists and Rafters, 4 x 2 Pine.
Flooring, 6½ x 1 T. & G. Pine and 4 x 1 Dressed Hardwood.
Sheeting to exposed Walls, 6½ x 1 Pine Chamfer Boards.
Sheeting to Walls under Verandah and Partitions, 4½ x 1 T. G. V. Pine.
Lining to exposed Walls and Ceilings, 4½ x ⅝ T. G. V. Pine.

Ceiling to all rooms. Scotia to ceilings. Fillets to floors. Panel doors inside, with fret panels over. Six French lights with fanlights over. Ledged doors to kitchen and verandah room. Windows as shown of clear glass. Galvanised iron roofing, ridge capping, spouting, down-pipe, stove recess, and stump caps. Berger's B.P. Paints (prepared) and brushes for three coats externally. Locks, hinges, fittings, anchor bolts, nails, solder, etc. Materials for E.C. 5ft. x 4ft., walls 7ft.; framing fitted. Materials for 1,000-gallon tank and stand.

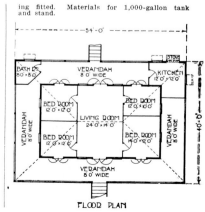

FLOOR PLAN

Inadequate supplies of local building materials and skilled labour in remote locations encouraged construction of a variety of pre-fabricated, light-weight houses which could be easily transported from major centres *to smaller settlements. Australian manufacturers followed the earlier practice of 19th century Victorian industrialists in England who produced a wide range of light-weight structures for shipment abroad.*

MINERS COTTAGES

The forerunner of northern Queensland's light-weight timber and iron dwelling is a standard miner's tent. It has been suggested that this tent was originally introduced from other colonies of the British Empire where it was a standard shelter of the British army personnel. On some mine sites in northern Queensland, where there were signs that mineral resources might last a little longer than previously envisaged, the workers decided to graduate from the flimsiest shelter to somewhat more permanent single-roomed timber framed cottages, whose walls and roofs were lined with corrugated galvanised iron sheets. In the fierce northern tropical sun, these single-roomed shelters proved far too hot for comfort, so it became a common practice to put another tin roof over the original cover, leaving a sizeable air-gap in between the two layers.

In Mount Isa one can see a typical example of this kind of structure, which has been well preserved by the local branch of The National Trust.

In Charters Towers and some other mining towns of northern Australia, which established reasonably permanent populations, these single-roomed cottages expanded to become two or even four roomed structures shaded by a three metre deep front and back verandah. In time, some of the owners added interesting embellishments in the form of decorative window metal hoods and brackets with stylised foliage design verandah timber posts. This development continued until the 1900s when many northern Australian towns could boast enormous mansions with four to six rooms accessible through a central corridor with all the rooms opening onto a continuous deep verandah which wrapped around the main structure. The growth of most of these large and luxurious houses generally coincided with the height of the mining boom.

This very old Mount Isa dwelling displays a completely separate iron roof. It is supported by a light-weight timber frame.

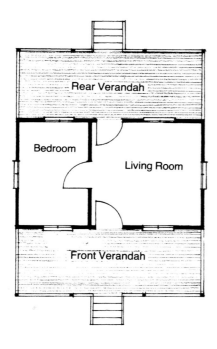

Plan of a very basic timber two-roomed miners cottage in Charters Towers, north Queensland.

Plan of a timber two-roomed miners house which expands upon the basic design with the addition of a kitchen, accessible from the rear verandah.

This two-roomed miners cottage in Charters Towers is a logical development of the single-roomed structure illustrated left.

The deep, front verandah of this simple miners cottage is surrrounded by a latticed screen, providing a cool, well ventilated living area.

13

INTRODUCTION

URBAN HOUSES

The enormous growth of primary industries in the inland areas led to the establishment of a string of large coastal cities which acted as the main outlet for export of regional products to the other parts of the world. Many coastal towns developed important secondary and tertiary industries which employed a considerable workforce and which, in turn, led to the concentration of substantial populations in these towns. Houses in these towns reflected the growing prosperity of the region and they were therefore much more elaborate than those in the mining towns further inland.

An important development which differentiates urban houses in the coastal towns of tropical Australia is the way suburbs follow the undulating topography where houses, large and small, are intermixed according to a fairly set pattern. Large houses of the rich are normally built on top of the ridges while those of the middle classes and workers follow down the hills into the valleys and low-lying flat plains below.

This pattern is clearly typified by the city of Brisbane where the history of segregation of houses according to status along the strip of hills is quite different from the kind of segregation one finds in other cities, such as Melbourne where, due to its flat topography, it is possible to draw a definite line between the richer and the poorer residential suburbs of sizeable proportion around the centre of the city.

Like most early settlements in Australia, Brisbane's central city and fringe areas were first densely populated, with the well-to-do occupying a few large estates on top of the nearby hills and the workers cottages situated on small allotments sprawling in the hollows of such areas as Spring Hill and Red Hill.

In the 1880s, due mainly to massive immigration, Brisbane's population jumped to well over 100 000 people, which added a great many new suburbs to the city. This trend continued until the turn of the century when everyone moved out of the city area leaving it entirely to business and commercial enterprises. This suburban expansion was further encouraged by introduction of faster public transport in the form of trams and railways, which extended radially, encouraging a sort of strip development away from the city centre.

The earlier pattern of segregation of houses of the rich and the poor was often repeated, with gracious large homes built on generous land on the tops of ridges offering a dramatic contrast to the small cottages of workers built on tiny allotments of 16 perches or less in narrow streets down the slopes and valleys.

In addition to marvellous views, hill-top houses enjoyed the cool breeze which was most welcome in the warm humid tropical summers. There were no proper water-borne sewage systems, so the houses down the slopes were not only denied the cool breezes but were also forced to receive the effluent from above!

Although developers are doing their best to demolish all traces of old style houses in Brisbane, there are still many good examples of large, medium and smaller houses left to give the city a distinctive character which is not evident elsewhere.

Because of the narrow frontage of the allotment, the side verandahs of this small four-roomed house in Brisbane have been omitted.

Plan of a four-roomed workers cottage in the Brisbane urban area. Its basic structure is similar to the North Queensland miners cottage.

The placement of verandahs at the sides or back depended both upon the shape of the allotment and the finances available for additions. A gable could be added to the cottage to provide extra room.

Right *These houses, situated on the tops of ridges in a Brisbane inner city suburb, are positioned to enjoy panoramic views and cool breezes.*

A MATTER OF STYLE

Tropical Australian houses offer an extensive variety of building types, ranging from small one to two roomed workers cottages to enormous mansions, well shaded with deep verandahs. Because of the limited range of materials and building crafts employed in the construction of these houses, there is a consistency of form evident throughout the region. This consistency was further reinforced by tradesmen and builders who widely employed pattern design books which were also familiar to the general public who knew what they wanted in the way of variations and embellishments to the standard plans.

Although no serious study has been done to categorise the forms of houses according to various architectural historical periods, it is possible to broadly group them according to various characteristics evident during the colonial, Victorian and Edwardian eras stretching from 1850 to 1920.

A city which has successfully managed to preserve these styles in a reasonably authentic manner is Ipswich, near Brisbane. In fact the whole city is a veritable museum for such a rewarding study. A glimpse of what is there has been admirably recorded by The National Trust of Queensland which, in *Ipswich: A Townscape Study*, has listed the various architectural styles of this fascinating city, some examples of which have been listed here.

It has been suggested by many historians that the standard plan form of a typical tropical house, which consists of four to six rooms juxtaposed back to back or linked through a corridor, had its basis in the Georgian buildings in the United Kingdom familiar to early settlers in Australia. These styles were transplanted in Australia with a verandah added as a concession to the local climate so that the walls could be shaded.

By 1840, when free settlers were allowed to settle in Moreton Bay, this modified Georgian style was already well established in New South Wales. Early settlers in tropical regions adopted these plans and appropriately modified them using timber more extensively rather than stone and brick as a main construction material.

However, according to Peter Bell, a major boost to the development of the kinds of buildings which finally evolved really occurred from 1860 onwards when the European settlements in northern Australia were backed by the industrial system. This system was proficient in manufacturing buildings which were derived more from the production requirements of the factory than the site. Perhaps this accounts for Mr Bell's assertion that 'local climate and indigenous materials have played little or no significant role in the development of these houses', rendering as he put it 'the whole concept of vernacular housing in the region questionable'. This extreme assertion of Bell may be arguable, but it is certainly true that this factory influence was not present in colonial domestic architecture in other parts of the world.

A parallel is often drawn between the Australian tropical house and the Indian bungalow (which was extensively built by the English during the colonial period of the eighteenth and nineteenth centuries). It was a European version of the Bengal double roofed house which, like its Australian counterpart, has four to six rooms back to back surrounded by a deep verandah. Also, like the Australian tropical homestead, the early bungalow was a convenient solution to a practical problem. It was cheap, quick to build and suitable for hot climates. However, once accepted, its temporary materials were replaced by more permanent materials, such as fired bricks, masonry columns and tiled roofs. Thus, a simple primitive Indian dwelling was later transformed into a system widely adopting many of the forms of neo–classicism.

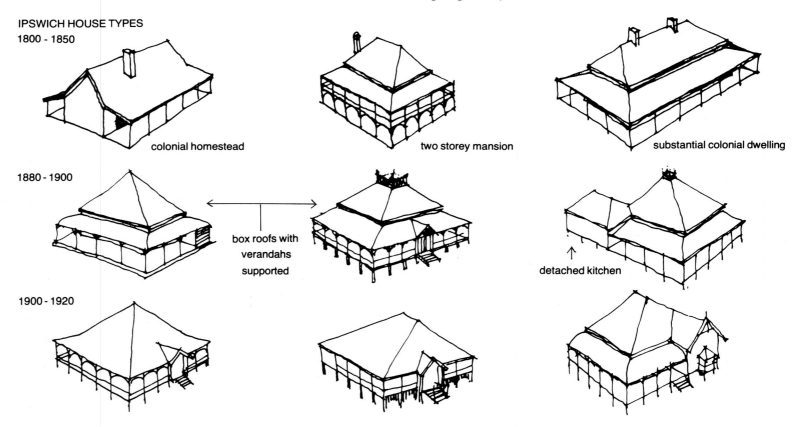

IPSWICH HOUSE TYPES

1800 - 1850

colonial homestead two storey mansion substantial colonial dwelling

1880 - 1900

box roofs with verandahs supported detached kitchen

1900 - 1920

An elegant Toowoomba house built during the late 1800's. A triangular pediment signifies the main entrance, breaking the verandah's uniformity.

The single-storeyed colonial bungalow such as this example from Cochin, India, inspired similar structures in other tropical colonies.

This brick and tile farm house, near Amidale, bears a remarkable similarity to the Indian bungalow of the 19th and early 20th centuries.

This typical, single-storey Dutch colonial house in Bandung, Indonesia, has a tiled roof, with vents for expelling hot air from the interior.

A prefabricated iron, steel and timber house in Broome, currently used as a court house. Its deep verandah is supported on cast iron columns.

Below *Oak Alley, a well preserved example of a French colonial plantation house in New Orleans, built in the early 19th century.*

During the nineteenth century this bungalow was built in various shapes and in different parts of the world, but in the beginning it stood out as the specific contribution of the Bengal Engineers to the cottage architecture of romanticism. One can see excellent examples of 'bungalows' in the Dutch colonies of Indonesia and in the Caribbean. The Spanish colonists in the south-western parts of the United States developed a building style which is very similar to the Caribbean and uses the adobe materials employed by the American Indians.

However, some of the most interesting examples (where French influence was very marked) can be found in a number of plantation houses along the Mississippi River in New Orleans in the State of Louisiana in the United States. Constructed on a grand scale, they epitomised the generosity and wealth of an era when land was plentiful, family groups were large and periodically added to by relatives, dependents and friends.

Architecturally, the classical Greco-Roman styles emphasised by the columns of these houses follow the important public buildings of the day when people took great pride in carving little empires of their own thousands of kilometres away from their ancestral origins.

All of these eighteenth and nineteenth century colonial domestic buildings had one thing in common. Their builders, whether they were British, Dutch, French or Portuguese, wanted to keep the memories of their mother countries alive; and so their preferences for certain prototypes were quite discernible and often carried strong undertones of sheer indulgence!

However, one important way in which these colonial houses were different from their counterparts in tropical Australia, was that the building materials used in these houses were largely masonry and therefore had a considerable heat storage capacity. This had a great advantage in hot dry climates as these materials took a long time to heat up during the day and therefore provided pleasant cool interiors.

This, and other related phenomena, is best explained when we examine the tropical climate to determine how its various elements such as heat, humidity, breezes and radiation from walls, floors and ceilings affect physical comfort. When we add these up, we get some idea of how a building is likely to perform in a specific location.

Medical science tells us that the human body is very much like an engine which obtains its energy from food. In a healthy person this is converted into heat which must be sufficient to maintain body temperature at 98.4°F. Any excess must be eliminated and this is done by radiation, conduction, and evaporation through air blowing on a sweaty skin and respiration. When this heat loss is faster than the production of heat within the body, we feel a chill. On the other hand, when the heat is produced faster than we are able to lose it, then we feel hot.

The human body is able to adjust itself to changes over a fairly wide range of conditions. When it is able to do so without strain, we describe ourselves as feeling very comfortable. The degree of comfort varies for differing circumstances and is affected by the character of the climate, type of clothing we wear and change and type of physical activity, and also the degree to which we have acclimatised ourselves.

In order to keep cool when it is very warm, the body

has to lose heat by evaporation in the form of sweat. In a dry climate this is relatively easy, but under humid conditions it is very difficult and the moist air is much more pleasant than the dry air at the same temperature. This is why most of us find the hot dry climate more acceptable than the warm humid one. It is also why, in more humid climates, air movement across the body is essential for comfort since it helps evaporation and cooling.

Clothes are a great help in maintaining the heat balance of the body. The traditional white and loose robes of the Arab, for instance, protect him from the sun's rays. They also provide insulation from the hot desert air, and against the cooler nights. At the same time they allow an unlimited amount of air to circulate freely over the surface of the body. On the other hand, in a warm and wet climate, the sun is less intense than in the desert areas. In addition, trees and vegetation offer shade. People in such regions, for example the Polynesians and the Melanesians, require little or no clothing from the point of view of comfort.

Tropical Australia has broadly two types of climates. Its north-eastern coastal regions are warm and humid and their soakingly wet atmosphere changes little by night and day. On the other hand its vast interior has a hot, dusty and dry climate. During summer, day and very often night temperatures stay persistently hot, but winter nights are cool with temperatures dropping to almost zero. Vegetation in such areas is sparse and stunted.

In contrast to the ruggedness of some early colonial houses, the elegant details of this tropical Australian house display a light, airy quality achieved with the versatility of timber and metal.

The clothing of early European visitors to hot climates, unlike that of the indigenous peoples, made little concession to the environment. It tended to be dark, heavy and comparatively tight-fitting.

This two storey, early 19th century Indian bungalow reveals overlays of Portuguese, Dutch and local building styles. Surrounded on three sides by verandahs, interior rooms are partitioned by carved teak screens.

19

CLIMATE

The vital question is how effective is the tropical Australian house in a region which has both hot dry, as well as hot wet climatic areas. The answer has to be negative. Light-weight, and what some people may term 'flimsy' materials, possess little or no barrier to heat penetration. If it were not for the verandah which shades the walls, living in these houses would be virtually unbearable.

In hot dry regions, materials which have high capacity for storing heat perform better because they take a long time to absorb most of the heat received during the day (before it is passed on to the inside surface). Therefore, houses with thick mud or brick walls are very cool during the day. At night, when the outside air is cooler, the inside rooms often remain too warm for comfort. The answer is to open all the doors and windows and let the cool air in. It is interesting to observe how people in desert settlements in North Africa or Western Asia, for instance, manage this problem. They simply move out of their houses at night to live and sleep outdoors, in courtyards, verandahs or roofs.

So it is easy to see why the Australian house fares so badly in this kind of environment. Not only are its walls and roofs insufficiently heat-proof, but, except for its verandahs where at least there is a little breeze, there is nowhere to escape during the stifling hot summer afternoons. Some ingenious families simply go out and sit under a tree or go into what is called a 'spinifex cool house'. This is an outbuilding constructed from clumps of spinifex grass fixed to a chicken wired enclosure which is continually sprayed with water.

The Australian house fares much better in warm and humid regions simply because the outside air temperature, though quite warm, generally remains reasonably steady during the day and night. Although day temperatures in these regions are not as high as one finds in inland areas,

the houses still tend to get pretty hot unless suitable attention is paid to proper orientation and shading devices.

Because of high humidity in such climates it is necessary to allow good cross ventilation so that people can feel the uninterrupted flow of breeze across their bodies. The layout of Australian houses, however, does not assist in this as rooms are usually juxtaposed back to back or linked to an internal corridor (rather than placed alongside each other in a single long row). Often, like many of those in the Pacific islands, houses are raised on stumps above ground to catch the breeze, but even here the problem of cross ventilation remains. The net result is that rooms of these houses largely remain unoccupied or at best become storage rooms, while the surrounding verandahs turn into living and sleeping areas. The latticed verandah, although it mellows the strong sunlight, provides little or no protection against wet season rain, which is usually driven in by strong winds. If it rains frequently or non-stop, then the only alternative is to either get thoroughly soaked or let down canvas blinds which, in turn, stop the breeze altogether and compel everyone to swelter under hot and muggy conditions.

The question is, if the tropical Australian houses are so inadequate for the hot climates, then why do people continue to live in them? The answer to this perhaps lies in the belief that the form of shelter is only partly determined by the local climate, economics and available materials and building skills. A major and perhaps the most important contribution is made by cultural factors. To understand these factors, we should examine people's attitude to lifestyle, their perceptions, and the degree to which they are prepared to accommodate themselves to their surrounding environment.

Here it may be useful to spotlight the differences which exist between the lifestyles and attitudes of Aboriginal people and those of the Europeans, as it is in many ways fundamental to our understanding of the way the

Pacific islanders instinctively build light, open shelters (raised to catch the prevailing breeze), appropriate to the tropical environment.

TYPICAL LAYOUT OF A TRADITIONAL AUSTRALIAN HOUSE

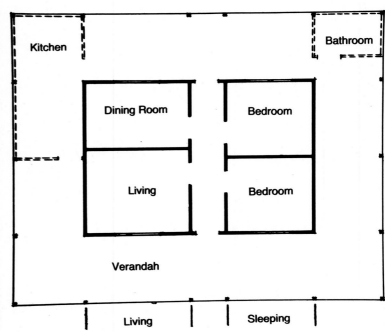

Kitchen

Bathroom

Dining Room

Bedroom

Living

Bedroom

Verandah

Living

Sleeping

The main rooms of a traditional timber house are juxtaposed back to back or accessible from a central corridor.

Australian tropical house has evolved over the last two hundred years. The early pioneers who came from Europe must have found Australia inhospitable and totally foreign to their historic experience. Coming from a world of long winters and reliable rainfall, they were confronted in Australia with a harsh land, 70 per cent of which was hot and dry country with not even a decent river system. So, they clustered in a few urban centres along the cooler and more temperate areas along the south-eastern fringe of this vast continent. They also brought with them the typical European attitude to nature which results in devising a shelter that treats a house as a barrier between them and their outside surroundings.

In fact, their is ample evidence that early Australians treated nature as their enemy rather than as a friend. It was harsh and unfriendly. It was something to be exploited rather than conserved.

The early European attitudes made no concession to the tropics. Their dress was inappropriate, with heavy, dark clothes providing covering to the neck. So was the food, which included a high intake of calories through meat. These attitudes later extended to working hours. Rather that allocating the hours of work to early morning and late evening, when it is cooler, the European practice of a nine to five working day was followed. These attitudes were also reflected in the early houses, which followed the European fashion of the time. The only concession was made by a verandah, about which more later.

In utter contrast to this were the attitudes and perceptions of the Australian Aboriginal people, who, as a result of evolution over thousands of years, had not only come to terms with nature but had learnt to live in total harmony with it. They have devised shelters and adopted a life and work style which ensures a balanced ecology and does least harm to the surroundings. An interesting difference which lies between the European and Aboriginal people is that the Aboriginal people tend to live *around* and not *in* houses. Perhaps it is their subsistence lifestyle itself which produces such behaviour.

So, it is clear that most people build houses which reflect their values and their attitudes to nature. While the early Europeans treated the house as a barrier between them and nature, the Aboriginal people saw it as a filter, or a sort of adjustable screen which incorporated, to some extent, their own flexible and adaptable attitude to the surrounding country. An Aboriginal has a very close physical and spiritual association with his country — something which was certainly missing among the early settlers.

But as the years passed the European attitudes began to change. Australia is perhaps one of the few tropical countries which the white man has learnt to accept as his permanent home. He has not only exploited the country to satisfy his physical needs, but also he, himself, has undergone a steady but subtle change. After nearly two hundred years of contact, a new Australian has been born who has steadily learnt to adapt to his land. His clothes are lighter, looser and less formal. Heavy and hot roast dinners have been replaced by salads and tropical sea food. There is more outdoor living and the chief recreation lies in thousands of Australians soaking up the sun on the surfing beaches along the extensive coastline which runs thousands

The verandah of this house in northern Queensland has been fully enclosed, the contrasting elements within the facade delineated by paintwork.

Because of inadequate cross ventilation, interior rooms are frequently vacated during the wet season in favour of the cooler verandah areas.

of kilometres around this vast continent.

This more relaxed attitude is also reflected in the houses, where much of life is spent on verandahs and other semi-enclosed areas which link the indoors with the outdoors. So, the Australian house may not provide all the answers to the rigours of the local climates, but it does reflect the attitudes and perceptions of Australians which have been considerably transformed over the years. These houses lend themselves to a more informal lifestyle, where people are not limited to shutting themselves indoors but may live around the house as much as inside it.

In this, the Australian has now become closer to his Aboriginal brother than ever before. There is a spirit of accommodation where he is prepared to adjust to his surroundings rather than turn his back on them. The house is not just a closed fortress alienated from its surroundings — but opens up and extends itself to grasp the hand of nature.

VERANDAHS

The most outstanding feature of the Australian house, the verandah, was primarily a response to climate. As time progressed, it came to fulfil a variety of functions. Shutters or blinds provided protection from the elements. Master craftsmen provided a decorative dimension with simple timber or more elaborate cast iron materials.

An important feature of the tropical house which encourages an informal, relaxed and open lifestyle is the verandah. When early Europeans settled in Australia, they transplanted building forms familiar to them in their home country. The basis of house designs was Georgian, a style well established in the United Kingdom.

Faced with long, hot summers, it did not take long for the early settlers to make appropriate modifications to allow for greater comfort by providing shade around the house. The first step was to extend the eaves which later became verandahs. Windows became larger to let in more breeze during the wet season.

There have been many guesses as to the origin of this verandah which later came to be accepted as a major feature of an Australian home. Some historians have suggested that it may have come from France via the North American colonies. Old American Midwestern towns are well known for their deep timber verandahs. Many two storey gracious American villas were distinctive for their tall verandahs which extended over both floors.

The most common belief, however, is that verandahs were introduced into Australia by officers who had served in India and in the Caribbean before establishing themselves in the new country.

Whatever its origin, the importance of verandahs as an architectural element in a tropical Australian house cannot be underestimated because it is one area which lent itself to an informal semi-outdoor lifestyle ideally suited to the climate. In the northern regions, verandahs invariably enclosed all four sides of a dwelling and often occupied more area than the 'house' itself which was limited to providing storage room for household possessions and some expensive items of furniture. Verandahs were used day and night and in some areas for the whole year. People used then for living, eating, sleeping and entertaining when guests could spill out into the garden during the long balmy summer afternoons and evenings. It was there that family reunions took place, when three generations would ritually turn up for Sunday barbecues at the grandparents'. Areas were set aside for drying clothes and as play areas for children.

A series of rhythmic arches, incorporated into the verandah of this utterly simple house in Maryborough, adds a highly individual note.

Right **Deep verandahs surround this house established early this century.**   Over **A verandah extension provides protection and informal living.**

VERANDAHS

So verandahs became an integral part of every house and their use an essential part of the Australian way of life. They offered a welcome refuge from the heat and glare of the piercing sun. The cool dark space framed with white posts and decorative balustrades became a symbol of the tropical house as an essential link between the indoors and the outdoors.

With so much use in the north-eastern regions where the sun was fierce and rain poured down in buckets, it became necessary to provide further protection for the verandah itself. So in places like Townsville and Charters Towers, one can see verandahs-on-verandahs, a sort of double extension to the roof to cut out the direct view of the sky and thus reduce glare and allow verandah users better protection from the sun and torrential rain. They were further protected by adjustable wooden shutters which could be closed during the cyclonic storms. Generally, verandahs were oriented towards the north-east and extended to the garden beyond.

The verandah-on-verandah, a sort of double extension to the roof, provides additional protection in north-eastern tropical regions. It cuts out a direct view of the sky, successfully reducing glare. The houses above demonstrate the resultant atmosphere of semi-outdoor living.

Adjustable shutters, screens or blinds (in timber or canvas) serve to shade the verandah by day and allow cool air to penetrate at night.

The erection of a partial screen at the front entrance provides privacy while allowing cool air to flow through the central corridor.

This unusual corner entrance has been constructed to suit the location of the house on the site. A portico defines the entrance.

Above and right **Light cane, timber or canvas furniture, informal and easy to move around, proved ideal for verandah use.**

VERANDAHS

When the early shingles were replaced by galvanised iron, special sheets were made for verandahs. At first they dipped in a slow graceful arc from below the eaves to the bressummer connecting the verandah posts. Later, when the verandahs became deeper, the metal sheets ran straight from below the eaves for three-quarters of their length and then dipped in a quadrant to the post line.

The form of early verandahs was fairly simple and direct, but later examples incorporated a variety of embellished features which took almost a bizarre form during the heyday of the Victorian era. The straight horizontal roof line of the verandah was invariably interrupted at the entrance to specially emphasise the link to the stairs. It was either a highly decorated triangular panel or a half-round section which sliced its way through the curved roof sheets like a barrel vault. The panels facing the main street were generally finished with elaborate timber or metal fretwork of designs directly derived from the natural surroundings of the house.

Compared to the somewhat uniform fenestration of the verandah, the entrance to this house in Ipswich is emphasised by a more elaborate treatment. Frangipannis frame the entrance.

The dual stairs leading to the verandah create an individual identity and add a touch of formality to an otherwise informal lifestyle.

The elaborate dual staircase of this house in Howard terminates in a covered porch which acts as a formal entrance to the house proper.

Right *The geometric design of the verandah is extended to the porch and staircase. The triangular pediment is a feature of the Rockhampton area.*

Pioneer builders often went to great lengths to emphasise the main entrance to counter the sometimes monotonous nature of the verandah facade. These highly decorated doorways and pediments are a testimony to their achievement, demonstrating the creative possibilities provided by timber.

The front panels of these pediments, designed in two sections, not only frame the panel behind but cast an intricate shadow pattern.

The timber and cast iron features of this house in Ipswich reveal a combination of textures and patterns.

The pediment has been fretworked from one solid piece of timber; its delicate lacework blends with the decorative treatment of the balustrade.

VERANDAH / *ENTRANCES*

These examples further illustrate the efforts of builders to break the monotony of the typical facade and create a point of interest. The highly decorated half-round timber sections were attached to the end of the barrel vault which was sheeted with curved galvanised iron.

A particularly robust version of the semicircular pediment of a barrel vault entrance which blends happily with the main roof.

The stable door proved a vehicle for further decorative treatment. The rising sun motif (left) reveals the influence of Chinese carpenters.

Interestingly shaped gable doors are capped with a simple pediment design which echoes the vertical decoration of the gables.

Glenbrae

Many of the highly individual features of what is essentially a basic cottage are embellishments handcrafted by the owner.

VERANDAHS

Somewhat stark verandah facades were also broken by trees and ornamental shrubs which were grown close to the balustrade. Deciduous vegetation was particularly welcome as it allowed the sun to penetrate during the winter and acted as a cool green shaded screen during the hot summers. In most cases this form of shading was insufficient, so the builders added a metre high balustrade of open slats or crossed trellis, and the space between the top rail and the eaves was encased in a variety of shutters and screens which could be adjusted to suit the climate.

When used for sleeping, the verandahs were enclosed with roll-up wooden shutters or canvas blinds for privacy. The more vulnerable aspects towards the east and west had full-height fixed trellis or wire screens (which allowed a lush overlay of leafy vines).

Right *The various elements of the verandah fenestration, while quite different in design and scale, are in total harmony with each other.*

This row of houses commands a panoramic outlook. Despite the general similarity of appearance, entrances and verandahs create variety.

Right *A well proportioned timber screen humanises the extreme height of this two storey structure, creating privacy for rooms at the upper level.*

VERANDAH / *SCREENS*

The latticed verandahs of these houses are surrounded by tropical vegetation. The screens provide a foil for shrubs and trees.

The partial lattice screening of these houses in suburban Brisbane provides privacy yet allows for free movement of air.

This trellis screens only that part of the verandah requiring privacy. It is non-structural yet accommodates itself well within the overall design.

A stained glass casement window (an unusual verandah feature) and adjustable timber shutters blend harmoniously within the structural framework. The variation of elements within the facade creates interest.

Over **This row of late 19th century cottages in Rockhampton, built for meatworkers, provides an example of durable, low cost building. The doorway provided one of the few possibilities for individual expression.**

Latticed screen envelops the entire length of the verandah and is incorporated into the doors at the entrance of this northern Australian house. Supplemented by lush tropical vegetation, it provides welcome shade, mellows the intense tropical light and ensures a continuous flow of cool air.

Screening to ensure privacy was vital for workers cottages which, on small allotments, were positioned close to the fence.

Right *Some of the charm of the traditional house derives from vegetation which surrounds the building, often penetrating the verandah area.*

VERANDAH / *SCREENS*

In an enclosed verandah situation, wooden shutters were able to adjust automatically to the pressures caused by cyclonic winds.

Adjustable wooden shutters (unlike contemporary venetian blinds used inside the window) both reduce glare and efficiently alleviate heat penetration.

The wooden shutters have been successfully integrated with the verandah design above the balustrade of this house in Ipswich.

The floral design of the triangular pediment offers a welcome contrast to the geometric design of verandah screens and balustrades.

Full length adjustable screens encompass the verandah of this house in Charleville, built during the last quarter of the 19th century.

VERANDAH / *DECORATIVE TIMBER*

Timber is a versatile building material and covers a wide spectrum of weight, colour, strength and grain. It lends itself particularly to intricate carving. The circular form of the panel on the right provides a frame for a stained glass window, a distinctive feature of this house in Maryborough.

The clover-leaf design of the curved barge board enhances the pediment, such embellishments made possible by the availability of good timber.

Right **The decorative treatment of the vertical slats of the curved edge panel considerably enhances a very simple verandah.**

The verandah detail displays the individual stamp of a skilled craftsman. The extraordinary swoop of the curve reveals the versatility of timber.

Triangular panels of carved timber employ motifs derived from Australian plants. The crown motif on the right reveals traditional allegiances.

The design vocabulary of this panel has been extended to incorporate the Australian heraldic motifs of kangaroo and emu.

This triangular timber panel displays a delicate floral pattern. The panel plays a dual role — it acts as a vent and reduces glare.

Verandah brackets incorporating floral designs provide a happy contrast to the straight geometric lines of shutters and blinds.

This bracket successfully solves the difficult problem of transition from post to verandah beam on one side and overhead panel on the other.

Decorative timber brackets also provide an effective screen to the mechanism which operates the adjustable timber blinds. Their designs provide a perfect foil to the austere lines of the blinds and effectively soften the total impression.

Verandahs of early timber houses were largely simple and utilitarian. However, in this example, the extra posts marking the entrance are decorative rather than structural. The utilitarian nature of the balustrade, posts and staircase is offset by the delicate curvilinear treatment of the brackets.

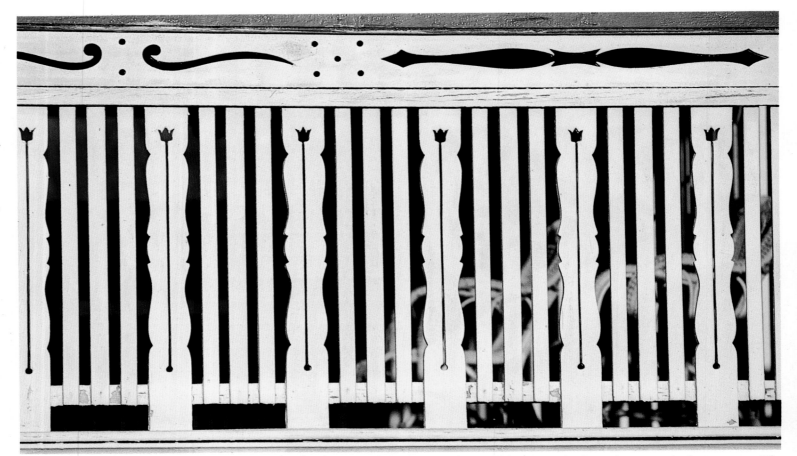

The vertical slats of this balustrade are intercepted at regular intervals by decoratively curved broad panels, thus achieving a rhythmic pattern. The slats are admirably balanced by a broad horizontal band which effectively emphasises the handrail above.

The timber balustrade of this Ipswich house is sturdier than that which is normally found in tropical houses. In its density it has become a dominant feature of the verandah. The posts are located closely to each other and therefore impart a strong verticality to the facade.

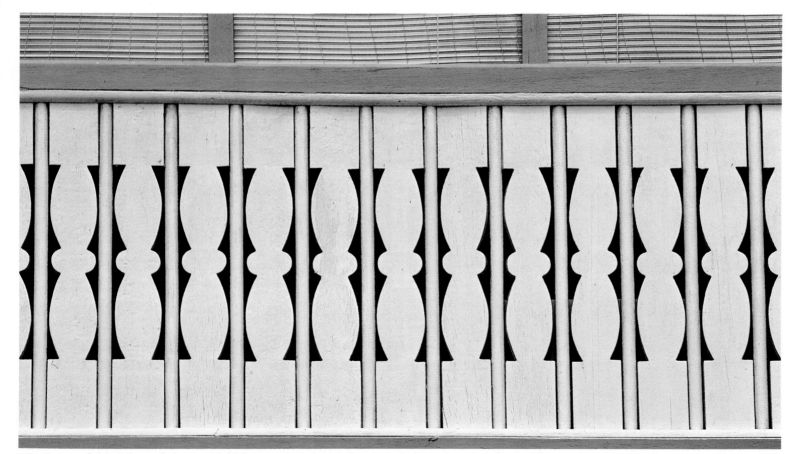

The design of this balustrade is an embellishment upon the regular vertical slat and tends to be two dimensional — yet it effectively harmonises with the screening above. The broad vertical members however do not allow as much air flow as those which are more narrow and set further apart.

Elegantly curved brackets harmonise with the slim posts below, displaying a masterly approach to posts located at awkward angles.

These Brisbane houses provide particularly novel examples of well designed timber brackets which link post and verandah beam.

The balustrade and brackets of this Toowoomba house combine to present a unified design.

This verandah furnishes an unusual variation upon a theme. Slim iron posts carry heavily decorated panels of cast iron.

The balustrades, however, lent themselves to a variety of decorative treatments where panels of cast iron tracery under the handrails of verandahs and external staircases added a welcome touch of opulence to what is otherwise a fairly stark and utilitarian building. The original panels, exclusively imported from the foundries in England, proved immensely popular with everyone, so much so that the Australian foundries jumped onto this lucrative market and began production on an extensive scale. They not only reproduced some of the original geometric patterns imported from overseas, but added their own designs which reproduced a great variety of forms derived from the Australian bush and wild life. The richness of these panels of native leaves, flowers, and wild life, included the kangaroo, emu and koala.

These designs were later carried to the tops of the columns which spread and opened up as fitting caps to the posts and embellished the underside of the verandah roof line. The use of the cast iron panels declined after World War I and has now been revived as part of the nostalgic return to the past, with its fine craftsmanship and intricate detail and its emphasis on individuality and elegance.

Cast iron balustrade, post, bracket and arch blend successfully. The effect is further enhanced by judicious use of colour.

53

VERANDAH / *CAST IRON*

  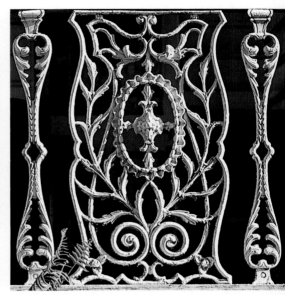

These cast iron balustrades display the wide variation in design possible. They were originally imported from England and proved most popular.

The popularity of the English product led to mass production in Australia when Australian motifs added considerably to the design vocabulary.

This cast iron balustrade provides a particularly rich example of a panel design inspired by local flora yet using traditional motifs.

THE HOUSE ON STUMPS

The house on stumps has long been regarded as a characteristically Queensland phenomenon. Whether the primary intention was to escape mosquitoes, white ants, heat or flood waters, the house on stumps has yielded both practical advantages and (when surrounded by timber panels or strips) further decorative possibilities.

To most people unfamiliar with the enormous range and variety of houses in the region, a northern Australian house conjures visions of a timber dwelling perched high on stumps. These stumps are usually hefty, round timber posts, creosoted to preserve them from pests and decay.

Statistically, the proportion of such houses is not high but, wherever they have been built, their unique form and character enables them to stand out prominently in what is often a drab and monotonous suburban landscape.

The phenomenon of the house on stumps developed fairly late in northern Australia. (Some historians have suggested that it occurred late in the nineteenth century.) On a flat site, the early pioneers built houses with floors either at ground level or 10 to 20 centimetres above it. Some floors were raised as high as 100 centimetres above ground. The stumps created just enough room to allow a person to crawl under the floor if necessary. Yet the floor was still too low for any effective use of this area. The introduction of the high-set house went beyond this and gave clear headroom for an adult. (It is classed separately from those houses which were designed and built as genuine two storeyed structures.)

A number of explanations and interpretations have been advanced as to the origins of the high stump house and the relative advantages of living in one. On a hilly site, building the house on stumps seems a rational and inexpensive way of obtaining a level platform. A more frequent advantage offered is that, by lifting these structures above the ground, it is easier for the owner to detect any white ant or borer infestation and take appropriate action.

Some owners, commenting favourably on the merits of the house on stumps, maintain that such houses are safely and conveniently positioned well above mosquitoes, snakes and cane toads; and that, further, they catch welcome cool breezes away from the thick vegetation at ground level. The latter explanation however makes little

The unique form and character of the house on stumps enables it to stand out prominently in what is often a stark, bare landscape.

sense on a flat site in an urban area where a concentration of houses on high stumps may effectively impede the flow of air throughout the neighbourhood.

It has been suggested that the height of stumps was increased in low-lying coastal and river flat lands in some country towns which were subject to periodic flooding. It did not take long, however, for their owners to realise that it was an economical way of doubling the available covered floor area. It became apparent that the extra space was most useful for drying clothes during the 'wet season'. This area was also a little cooler on summer afternoons as it was effectively insulated from the hot midday sun by the houses above it.

It became a favoured area for children, providing a sheltered play area, storage for toys and even an accommodation for pets. The extra space could also be adapted as a workshop, providing a relatively safe storage area for those tools and odds and ends necessary for a self-reliant family to survive in the open country.

The idea of building on high stumps, however, never really appealed to architects. Dodds, who is considered a significant figure in the field of tropical houses design and who used many traditional elements in his structures, found high stumps ugly and had some disparaging things to say about them.

Early high stump houses were brutally frank and their owners made no attempt to disguise their so-called forest of black columns. Later examples suggest that people found this 'nakedness' somewhat embarrassing and therefore tried to hide the stumps by surrounding them with panels of timber strips or some other decorative material. The effect, in many cases, was a little forced and the whole exercise invariably looked like an afterthought. All the same, it is also possible to find houses where such decorative treatment has been able to successfully achieve visual harmony with the rest of the structure, thus giving the impression of a double storeyed, well-knit and unified dwelling.

The stark forest of stumps was often relieved by a skirt of hardwood batten panels, in this instance softened with a decorative edge.

The art nouveau influence displayed in this skirting panel further reveals the design opportunities created by the house on stumps.

Right *The stumps and panels of this Brisbane house have been darkened to reduce bulk and provide a contrast to the house above.*

The vertical slats at ground floor level are a dominant feature of this house. Balustrade and staircase harmonise with the panels below.

Detail of a stump, offset with vertical slats, which displays the cap designed to prevent white ant infestation.

Panels in the form of simple arches are a common yet pleasing form of enclosure for the house on stumps.

This house, bare of decorative elements is an early example of the house on stumps. It provides shelter for drying clothes during the wet season.

The simple enclosure of the area beneath the house by diagonal slats has created a variety of possible uses, including storage and play areas.

ROOFS

Roofs provided a fundamental form of shelter and, by the mid-nineties, were constructed almost solely of galvanised iron. The early pyramid form was, in many instances, supplanted by the gable; ornate finials and vents provided further opportunity for variety.

Traditionally, in most hot humid parts of the world, the one building component which dominates above all else is the roof. The importance of the roof as a major architectural form is underlined by the need to shelter from the hot sun and rain. The walls are comparatively unimportant, except for reasons of privacy and security.

Samoan houses, locally known as *fales*, perhaps represent the ultimate in this approach. They are no more than pavilions on raised floors, where walls are entirely absent and the roof is supported on round wooden pillars. The interior (and thus all the household possessions, beds, storage cabinets and seating furniture) is all there on view; but nobody cares in a society which is more open than most others in neighbouring islands of the South-west Pacific.

In the Australian tropical house, the dominant feature is also the roof, which is basically a pyramidal core shape surrounded by a perimeter verandah. It is perched like a digger's hat casting welcome shade on everything below it.

In addition to the pyramid, there are at least three other forms — namely the modified pyramid, the straight gable and the multiple gable. Invariably, the verandah roof had its own character, often dropped below the main roof, either straight iron or gracefully curved near the edges. Some buildings went beyond the basics, experimenting freely with highly ornate shapes.

Apart from the verandah, the most visible component of a tropical house is its roof, as demonstrated by this Brisbane house.

Some of the early, simple roof forms were — with prosperity — replaced by the more elaborate, straight gable and multiple gable roofs.

Roofs of tropical houses consisted usually of a timber frame covered with sheets of galvanised iron, which could be easily transported.

Over *The roof is a major feature of this house near Ipswich. It is a prototype of a pastoralist's homestead of the 1890s.*

ROOFS / *VENTS*

The early roofing material of most buildings consisted of timber shingles which, by the mid-nineties, were replaced by corrugated galvanised iron. Its good qualities of lightness, strength and durability were well recognised, while furthermore it was weathertight, requiring little or no maintenance after construction. Being light, galvanised iron could be transported over long distances to remote construction sites at relatively low cost.

In hot humid coastal areas, chimneys are rarely found; although in the inland areas, where winter nights can be rather chilly, fireplaces are common. In early structures these fireplaces, like the houses themselves, were also constructed from timber but were detached from the main dwelling as a fire precaution.

When corrugated iron became available, it was used to line the inside of the fireplace and chimney. The floor was stone and ant-bed and fires were kept going continually to keep the house warm through the winter months. Some of the larger houses had more elaborate chimneys which used masonry material. However much

Chimneys are more commonly seen in the inland regions where temperatures are low in winter.

more attention was paid to the ventilators (which was understandable since they performed a very important function in expelling the hot air during the more severe summer period). So galvanised iron ventilators were a common sight and were available in a large range and in various sizes. The skill of the sheet metal worker was obvious. There were simple devices employed, such as curved blades which move as a result of wind pressure and act as exhaust for hot air fans inside the building.

Roof ventilators can be observed in a wide variety of forms which range from simple timber or metal panels to highly ornate sheet metal fixtures. Some ventilators display quite ingenious decorative variation which extends to ridge caps. They were available with dampers and removable screens.

Although there are exceptions, most ventilators are variations of a cylindrical fitting, capped with a conically shaped cover designed to keep out rain. The ventilators are sufficiently weathertight to withstand the cyclones and tropical storms of coastal northern Australia.

ROOFS / *VENTS*

Two examples of long, elegantly shaped vent fixtures which allow hot air to escape and create interest and variety in the roofscape.

This ornate roof vent (left) combines successfully with a weather-vane. The more common variety (right) is also widely used in industrial buildings.

Sheet metal workers were able to successfully manipulate the material in a variety of ways to suit specific areas of the house.

The decorative corner features, positioned at the joining of roof gutters, add an oriental dimension and relieve the abruptness of the gutter line.

ROOFS / *METAL WORK*

The metal roofs of traditional Australian houses present some difficult problems in keeping them cool during the summer. Metal is a good conductor of heat and, because of its orientation and comparatively large area, it is a major source of heat gain in the building. Hot sun beats down incessantly on the roof surface and, after passing the thin metal, heats up everything under it (including people, who literally swelter under this onslaught). There is no respite, except to move out onto the verandah or under the shade of a tree in the garden where at least the breeze may provide a bit of relief. Some scientists have recorded that air temperatures inside the houses during summer afternoons can be almost double those which prevail outside.

All this points to the need for some insulation, particularly at ceiling level. Early pioneers knew little about it and in fact it was considered somewhat 'sissy' to surround oneself with too much comfort. No wonder it took so long for even ceiling fans to be fully accepted in Australia at a time when these and other mechanical aids to

This elegant cast iron crown can be easily overlooked by passing motorists.

The roofs of tropical houses bear the brunt of the hot tropical sun and are therefore a major source of heat transfer into the house proper.

physical comfort were well established in most other parts of the tropical world.

Another sensible method which may be used to prevent the sun heating a metal roof is to paint the roof with light colours (preferably white, which is known to be an excellent deflector of heat). It is good to see more and more people covering the red roofs of their houses with white paint. It is now also possible to choose from a large range of insulation materials which can be laid just above the ceiling at a nominal cost.

Many ridge caps have been removed and not replaced by owners. They should be retained at all costs.

The pressed metal ridge cap terminates in an elongated timber finial.

Ridge embellishments contribute significantly to the local skyline.

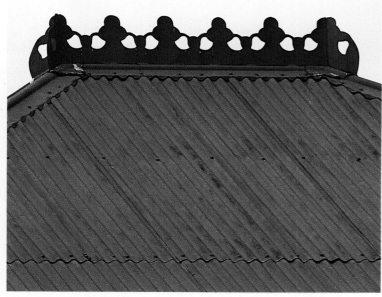

This pressed metal ridge decoration creates a dramatic silhouette.

This more restrained design adds definition to the ridge line.

Over *The basic roof form of an Ipswich house where the straight slope above the main rooms contrasts with the curvilinear verandah below.*

71

ROOFS / *AWNINGS*

Except for the south facade, all other walls of the house have to bear the brunt of hot tropical sun at some time or other during the day. As the north wall is particularly vulnerable during the hottest period, window hoods are a mandatory device for reducing the heat's intensity.

These galvanised iron window hoods display imaginative treatment. The hoods have been decorated both on their sides and fascias.

Decorated with circular motifs, this hood of a window on the north side is situated between the studs of an exposed exterior wall frame.

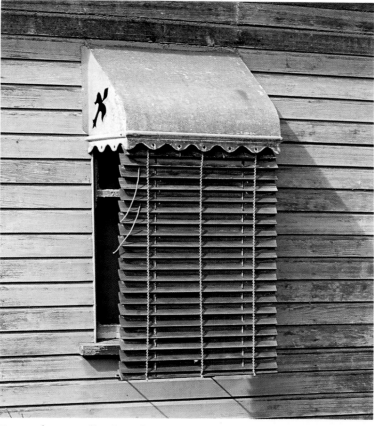

East and west walls of northern Australian houses receive early morning and late afternoon sun which necessitates supplementary shutters.

Shutters are most effective positioned outside the window as they prevent the sun beating down directly on the glass and generating heat. These adjustable shutters have been firmly attached (both to the front and to the hood and to the sill below) to stop them rattling in strong winds.

This attractive row of windows faces west, bearing the brunt of the afternoon sun. The internal venetian blinds are less effective than shutters.

Detail of a scalloped, shield-like motif decorating a window hood.

A series of carved brackets supporting light window hoods.

Right ***The well shaded window of a Townsville house, built in 1914. Literally handcrafted by its owner, this theme is carried throughout the house.***

A roof look-out, its balustrade matching the verandah below, was a common feature of the larger houses built during the late 19th century.

The distinctive conical roof, which incorporates a vented base, succeeds in emphasising the main entrance to this elegant Rockhampton house.

This example features a roof vent on a grand scale, filtering natural light to the main living area which would otherwise have been gloomy.

The octagonal roof terminates in an observatory, a light framed metal crown. It overlooks the flat townscape of Maryborough.

Right. *A particularly elegant roof, crafted in timber and metal.*

Over *Multiple gable roofs replaced the early pyramid form and were frequently punctuated by vents, chimneys and other embellishments.*

ROOFS / FINIALS

This simple ornament is most frequently used to finish the ridge cap.

A finishing edge face to the ridge cap of a house in Ipswich.

A triangular roof ventilator, capped by a highly ornate metal fixture.

Ventilated gables are invariably crowned by highly ornamental finials.

A particularly decorative finial which incorporates a weather-vane.

Although available in timber and terracotta, finials in particular provided the sheet metal workers with an avenue for self-expression.

Ventilated panels make provision for further decorative treatment.

The elegant finial to an Ipswich house, inspired by floral design.

An unusual example, as both ridge cap and finial are timber.

Geometric and floral motifs combine to create a distinctive roofline.

83

The end of the ridge cap has been formed in pressed metal, completing the design concept of this triangular gable with its separate pediment.

Widely spaced vertical slats at the verandah entrance create a welcome balance to the delicate floral design of a gable vent above.

The barge board of this triangular pediment which displays the rising sun motif has been fretworked from a solid piece of timber.

A more direct, functional answer to a gable vent capped by a finial. The simplicity of the diagonally placed slats is effective.

This gable vent provides another example of the rising sun motif which has been set within a rigid triangular timber frame.

To avoid the abrupt join between the roof overhang and the exterior wall below, ingenious builders have devised rows of carved wooden brackets which create a gentle, undulating effect.

The examples of bracket supports above display the extensive range and variety of design possible. In particular they reveal the malleable, sculptural qualities of high quality timber.

This roofline employs horizontal timber panels, gently curved and pointed, to provide a novel answer to the transition from the main roof of the house to the curved verandah cover below.

INTERIORS

Visitors to large Australian houses usually entered through an elaborate, timber front door surrounded by a stained glass panel of art nouveau designs and patterns. Further decorative elements were supplied by ornate timber brackets, panels and ceilings of pressed metal.

In an Australian tropical house, rooms as such are relatively less important than other sheltered and semi-sheltered areas around the core building (such as verandahs, terraces, and spaces under the shade trees which allow uninterrupted flow of breeze, but shield from the sun and rain). Consequently, in most workers cottages and middle-income dwellings, verandah furniture such as squatters chairs and light cane and timber seats and tables were more extensvely used than the more formal and heavy items popular during the Victorian era.

Large mansions of the well-to-do, however, were carefully furnished with good examples of what was generally known as the 'period furniture' imported from England. During the late nineteenth and early twentieth centuries, interiors of many Australian houses displayed the prevailing Victorian eclectic taste with well padded and elaborate sofa sets and dark stained timber chairs and tables surrounded by bric-a-brac of all kinds. Such heavy and padded furniture (which tends to wrap around the body) is highly unsuitable for tropical climates as it allows little or no air circulation around the skin. No wonder these rooms were rarely used by people who preferred light-weight open cane and timber furniture. It was easy to move it to a cool area and its design was such that it touched the human body at a very few points thus allowing a free circulation of currents of air for cooling.

The squatters chair has proved a durable item of verandah furniture.

A well protected verandah often receives more use than the interior.

Cane furniture, which is light and manoeuverable, has the advantage of allowing air to circulate freely around the body during sultry conditions.
Right *An elaborate door, framed by art nouveau stained glass panels.*
Over *Horizontal placement of weatherboard creates perspective and controls the visual scale of the hallway.*

INTERIORS

Most large houses had an elaborate timber front door surrounded by a stained glass panel of art nouveau designs and patterns. The main entrance led to a hallway, off which lay two large and important rooms. The hallway terminated in an enormous square or hexagonal drawing room well-lit from above by a high clerestory window. The transition from the hallway to this large drawing room was made less abrupt by highly ornate timber brackets which framed the top of the opening. This theme was also carried on to equally ornate and beautifully carved timber panels which topped all internal doors and which encouraged good cross-ventilation across the interior during the hot summer afternoons.

Another decorative element employed in the rooms lay in the elaborate designs of pressed metal ceilings of early houses which were often painted in a variety of colours. Ceilings of most tropical houses are, however, lined with a straight tongue and groove timber board. Mouldings of plaster and timber were profusely applied at cornices and around the wall and ceiling fixtures such as lights and fans.

This semicircular archway, consisting of a central disc with radiating panels, signifies the boundary between the hall and drawing room and makes the transition less abrupt.

The fretwork panel over the internal doorway allows constant airflow through the interior.

The formality of this entrance heralds a stately interior. A liberal use of timber is displayed in the heavily panelled door and decorative posts.

Right *This front entrance door with brass knockers and name plate is surrounded by art nouveau stained glass panels. Note the interesting relationship with the verandah ceiling above.*

90

INTERIORS

The use of colour enhances the ornamental moulding at the cornice.

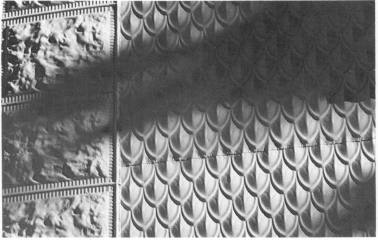

An early, decoratively patterned example of a pressed metal wall panel.

The glass panelled internal door filters light yet ensures privacy.

Detail of a stained glass panel with a floral motif. Such panels were a frequently used decorative element in doors and window frames.

In contrast to the bold, brightly coloured art nouveau designs, these glass panels add privacy, exhibiting patterns of delicate motifs and muted colours.

The use of stained glass, with its play of light and pattern, enriches the internal vista down the hallway, formalising the transition to the interior.

INTERIORS / STAINED GLASS

Stained glass panels have been used effectively in the row of windows (left) and the french doors with vent panel (right). They open up from formal living areas, providing both access and light. Both examples are an elegant statement of the art.

These windows provide an instant strip of light, the otherwise mundane view of the neighbourhood enlivened by the landscape in the central pair.

The most noteworthy feature of this room is the direct relationship of the living area to the verandah via french doors.

The rare example of a bay window adds a touch of elegance.

Detail of an art nouveau design to a window panel.

In the majority of tropical houses it is uncommon to find authentic period furniture such as that displayed in this Charters Towers study.

This elegantly furnished Charters Towers bedroom displays the mosquito nets widely used in insect-infested tropical regions.

This airy, traditional sitting room displays the pressed metal ceiling which was available in a variety of patterns.

Right *An example of an open, carved timber panel which underlines the transition between two rooms.*

FENCES

*The early European settler felt a pressing need to carve
out his bit of territory and so a variety of fencing materials evolved,
from simple timber or chain-link fences to more elaborate
pre-cut panels.*

In a vast continent such as Australia, where land was unlimited and nature untamed, the early European settler felt a pressing need to carve a bit of territory which he could call his own and on which he could put his individual stamp. This need led to fencing on a vast scale and this activity was given a further boost when the European system of land ownership was transplanted to the colonial soil. Boundaries were marked and, in the case of housing lots, simple chain-links or timber fences were considered adequate to keep animals out and children in.

Galvanised wire was easily available, so chain-link boundary fences became most common and were often combined with hedges. Later, timber paling fences proved most popular for screening front and side boundaries. They were generally a metre or so high and were either painted white or occasionally creosoted. Some manufacturers of building materials jumped on to this lucrative market and began supplying all kinds of fencing components (cut to lengths, with posts already mortised and rails already tenoned in a variety of designs and timbers).

Timber fences of larger houses were often higher and more elaborate. Some were close-boarded to provide better seclusion. Another variation was the horizontally boarded decorated fence where boards were spaced several centimetres apart. A few builders even introduced pre-cut and assembled panels which were close-boarded or with slats interwoven, lapped horizontally or spaced.

These themes were carried on, both to the designs and heights of gates, which matched the fences and were invariably constructed with more ornate patterns and decorative embellishments. However, very few of the gates supported both the number and house name plates. The house name plates were generally located in a prominent position in the front porch or the verandahs.

Although high timber fences were often erected for added privacy, most owners relied less formally upon hedges and shrubs.

As galvanised wire was easily acquired, the chain-link fence was a com-mon form of fencing, later modified to incorporate timber components.

Over **Later, timber paling fences proved a popular screen for front and side boundaries, harmonising well with timber frames and balustrades.**

The pavilion to the right of this house in Rockhampton extends right into the garden, providing uninterrupted views of trees, shrubs and flowers.

Tall palm trees provide a striking frame to this large, tropical house in Rockhampton edged by a traditional painted timber fence.

Right *The trees and shrubs of this old house have taken many years to grow and are now an integral part of the tropical ambience.*

Over *The stark effect of lattice and vertical slats is offset by a luxuriant frame of foliage and trees, creating a cool and shady oasis.*

This low timber fence serves more as a territorial boundary and does not attempt to hide the tropical vegetation which dominates the setting.

A simple picket fence surrounds this Charters Towers house, its vast verandah screened by a balanced combination of windows and shutters.

An example of an elaborate timber paling fence which blends well with this fine example of carpenter's Gothic in South Townsville.

This gate to a house in South Townsville has been almost hand crafted and is reminiscent of the tori of a Japanese Shinto shrine.

This view from the front verandah exhibits the versatility of timber and the endless possibilities it creates for an imaginative designer.

FENCES

Generally a metre or so high, the turned paling tops, fixed (left) in undulating lines, relieve the harshness of a horizontal line.

The more open and geometric pattern of this fence is quite rare and is derived from the decorative framework used in the single-skinned house.

During the early period of the development of northern Australia, the primary function of a fence was to keep animals out and children in.

The height and design of the gate usually incorporated the basic theme of the fence although occasionally gates were of more ornate construction.

This traditional, spear-headed picket fence, while somewhat dilapidated, has a certain charm.

Detail of a panel in the timber gate of a house in Rockhampton.

Timber slats, carved at the top, create a more decorative linear effect.

The verandah of this house shows a particularly innovative yet functional use of lattice screening which extends even to windows and doors.

Nostalgia was reflected in house name plates which listed such names as Lavenham, Glenbrae and Dumfries. While some owners chose such exotic names as Torre and Nyleta, many used Aboriginal names such as Oonooraba and Boondah as a more direct association with their adopted land.

RESTORATION & RENOVATION

The restoration and renovation of a traditional timber house requires a basic understanding of this form of domestic architecture. The original charm of interiors, verandahs, roofs and gardens can, with discernment, be retained and happily accommodated to the requirements of contemporary life.

For those buyers or owners of old tropical houses who believe that their home has some historical significance, there are some excellent guidelines available from the nearest branch of the National Trust. But, before starting, the features requiring restoration should be carefully noted. It is necessary to establish where possible the year the house was built and by whom, which materials and structural systems were used originally and what changes, if any, have been made to the building during its life span. Such information is very useful in restoring missing details.

The first step is to gather the relevant information from official (mainly local authority) records, titles, building permits, formal papers such as letters, diaries and newspaper reports and old photographs, and other available sources. If there are problems in obtaining this information then one may have to resort to secondary, and therefore less accurate, sources such as later publications, verbal comments of old folks in the neighbourhood or simply direct comparison with other similar structures in the vicinity, records of which may be available. The whole operation is somewhat tedious but rewarding as it could result in an authentic, well-restored house which is in close sympathy with the concept of its earlier occupiers.

The National Trust of Queensland recommends a three-stage operation which includes getting hold of real property description, search of title and a browse through old Post Office Directories. Real property description, which includes parish and allotment or section or sub-section, can be obtained from the rate notice or from the rate department of the local authority. Title documents which indicate sequence of owners and which are normally identified by volume and folio numbers, are held in state government offices. Once details of title and real property description have been acquired, it is profitable to browse through old Post Office Directories. These directories often yield information about the early residents, streets, suburbs, towns or districts, all of which may assist in determining the origins of an old house. Such directories are normally available for reference from State Libraries such as the Oxley in Brisbane and Mitchell in Sydney.

The restoration of a traditional house is a labour of love and it can be an expensive exercise unless a watchful eye is kept on the costs of labour and materials involved. The aim should be to restore it as closely as possible to its original style; but in a house which has to be constructed and used by its occupiers, it is often impractical to restore it entirely to its original form as a sort of a museum piece. After all, we have come a long way since our grandmothers used wood stoves in the kitchen, and the family washed in the bedroom or verandah by splashing water from a hand basin and a jug.

It is important to make a list of priorities and decide which are the most important features requiring restoration without compromise. Missing items should be replaced by carefully detailed copies, the designs of which match the original. Similarly, materials should be cut to the same size and form as those being replaced. Old timber houses generally relied more on jointing and less on nails and other modern short cuts. Restoration should follow such techniques and joints should be preserved and reproduced where necessary. So look out for carpenters and joiners who can do this kind of work. If a particular material or technique is historically significant but is unacceptable to local building authorities as it fails to comply with current regulations, then a well-documented appeal should be made to waive application of such rules. To do this, it is useful to record the existing structure in the form of measured drawings so that a good case can be clearly and more accurately made. During renovations and restoration work, it is also important to store all the left-over bits and pieces of old timber joinery and ironmongery for possible re-use elsewhere in the same house, as it all helps to maintain the original theme and character of the structure.

Utility rooms, such as kitchens and bathrooms, can be 'modernised' by using new fixtures and finishes which are sympathetic to the rest of the structure. Generally, natural materials such as timber sit more happily than plastic or aluminium sheets. Some of the rooms may also have to be used for purposes other than those for which they were originally planned and this will further necessitate some minor modifications.

The importance of adhering to the original design concept is perhaps more relevant to buildings which have been classified by the National Trust as essential to Australia's heritage. Some general principles for restoration have been laid down by the International Council on Monuments and Sites (ICOMOS). According to these guidelines, restoration means returning the existing fabric of a building to a known earlier state. It is only appropriate if there is sufficient evidence of this earlier state and if restoration to that state is likely to enhance the cultural significance of the building.

The Council warns that it is not desirable to embark on restoration work unless adequate resources are available. If properly executed, restoration should reveal culturally significant aspects of a building and should be based on respect for all the physical, documentary and other evidence. Restoration should stop at the point where conjecture begins.

Although ICOMOS guidelines are quite helpful in a general way, in most cases, the advice of a sympathetic architect may be adequate. A list of such professionals who are knowledgeable in or specialists in restoration programmes can be obtained from the local branch of the National Trust (who usually help with an up to date register of such services).

In all building programmes concerned with restoration or renovation, the important step is to thoroughly examine the work, establish its style, understand the way in which it was built and the process required to restore it (at all times resisting the temptation to add preconceived notions of 'improvement', which may detract from the aesthetic appeal of the original). This may also involve the need to ignore the fast-talking salesman of building materials and components which appear to offer short cuts at the expense of quality.

Successful renovation involves a happy harmonising of traditional and new features.

Much of the appeal of verandahs was lost when owners began to board them up to gain more enclosed living space. Removal of such enclosures often reveals beautiful timber features.

After all, nineteenth and early twentieth century builders in Australia obviously knew what they were doing. They have left a fine legacy of good building of which we can all be proud. Some of the hand-crafted building techniques are just as valid today as they were 150 years ago and we should not be ashamed of using them if they help us to effectively restore our heritage.

An area in which the traditional Australian house offers many lessons lies in the realm of those creative endeavours which have been associated with such light-weight materials as timber and metal sheets. These materials are easy to manipulate and ideally lend themselves to a rich and unlimited variety of expression. Anyone with simple tools can make such decorative elements as column brackets, panels and screens with fretwork. It is possible to envisage a new backyard craft industry which could be richly rewarding. This kind of activity is particularly relevant to an era in which there is likely to be more leisure time available.

EXTERIOR

Appearances can be deceptive, so carefully check all the important features of a house.

The most obvious component which deserves a careful examination is the roof. It is invariably of corrugated iron and, if located in hot and humid regions, is most likely to have rusted beyond repair. Any replacement should involve careful consideration of the original character which should be preserved as far as possible. This means it is necessary to avoid the temptation to use more sophisticated sheet materials, unless they closely resemble the old. Sheet steel has replaced much of the old iron roofing material yet there are some colours, such as 'gull grey', which are very similar to an old well-weathered iron roof. New sheets are also available in long lengths which means fewer laps and hence less chance of leaks and rusty edges. However, use of long lengths could well alter the scale of the old roof which was partially dictated by smaller sheet lengths and which, if critical, should be carefully followed during the restoration work. It is important to extend this sympathetic approach to other items such as traditional half-round gutters which should be replaced by quadrant or D-gutters.

The early houses on stumps were brutally frank and their owners made no attempt to disguise their so-called forest of black columns.

UNDER THE HOUSE

A look around the grounds of the house provides an opportunity to check the likely direction of the storm-water flow from the neighbour's backyard. It is possible that this flow may well end up on the site of the house under examination, thus causing a drainage problem which must be attended to as soon as possible.

Water-clogged soil near old tropical houses can loosen the ground around the round timber stumps and thus make these supports insecure for the house itself. Any real damage to stumps is difficult to assess since much of it is buried underground and cannot be ascertained without actually digging the soil (an activity not often welcomed by the seller or the real estate agent). However there are alternatives. The odd concrete stump normally means the floor has been re-levelled and minor repairs have been done to the under-floor structure at some stage.

All this can be reassuring, but it is equally possible that repairs may have been done many years ago and that further settlement may have taken place in the intervening period.

Signs of packing and gaps between the tops of stumps and bearers clearly indicate that some stumps have sunk and packing suggests makeshift levelling. Another danger sign is a rim of decayed timber near the ground level. In any event, the need for stump repair (or in severe cases complete re-stumping) does not mean a major calamity. Most old timber homes do pose this problem and the extra cost of repairs involved should be taken into account.

Because of a long history of neglect and the need for periodic maintenance, there seems to be considerable prejudice against round timber stumps. Many owners increasingly prefer concrete or steel supports, which is a great pity since timber stumps are nowadays pressure treated and certainly look more appropriate for a traditional tropical house.

While examining under the house it is also important to check for white ants above the ant-caps, for infestation may well extend through the whole house. In case of minor damage it may only be necessary to replace a few affected members and replace ant-caps. However, major damage can involve costly repairs.

Unduly moist conditions and poor ventilation are a major cause of decay. Leaky waste and water pipes are a major offender. Rot sets into the timber which then has to be replaced. Further plumbing repairs and improvements to ventilation are necessary to avoid further damage.

The impact of termites and decay is not limited to bearers and joists only but also extends to the floor boards (which must be carefully checked, particularly if they are cunningly hidden under a newly laid carpet). The most vulnerable areas are under the kitchen sink, the bathroom, and the laundry (if it happens to be upstairs).

Second-hand and demolition building material yards often sell good pine flooring to replace the rotten pieces and match the existing floor. Using second-hand hardwood is pointless because it is nearly always impossible to drive nails through it. Many carpenters simply refuse to work with old hardwood. On the other hand, new timbers do not often exactly match the old.

Floors are usually tiled after they have been properly levelled, otherwise they are likely to crack when the house is jacked up to level it. Even the hardwood underlay is liable to crack under such circumstances.

RAISED FLOOR

An important characteristic of tropical Australian houses is that many of them have been raised off the ground on round timber posts (which could be varied according to the slope of the ground) to provide a flat floor surface effectively and cheaply. Later this method was also applied to houses on flat land because it was an economical way to achieve additional covered space for a variety of uses. A frequent explanation given is that by raising the floor it is easier for the owner to detect any white ants and take appropriate action before too much damage is done to the structure. It is doubtful whether this is the main reason. A more realistic assessment probably recognises the real gains in additional covered area with little extra cost. The space is very useful since it is one of the coolest areas in summer and children and their friends can play while their parents are involved with the washing and other household chores. The space is also used as a store, workshop and as a carport.

Houses on high round timber posts were built fairly late in northern Australia. The earliest examples had floors at either ground level or 10 to 20 centimetres above it. Some were raised as high as 100 centimetres but were still too low for effective use. High set houses went beyond this and gave clear headroom for an adult. Classed as separate from those which were designed and built as genuine two storeyed structures, these houses were first built in and around the hilly terrain of Brisbane and were later adopted for building in northern areas from 1890 onwards. Although many architectural historians consider these houses as typical examples of tropical building in northern Australia, statistics suggest that the bulk of the houses in this region are fairly low.

In this example, the raised floor has been successfully disguised by a curved skirting panel which echoes the vertical lines of the balustrade. With restoration, it is important to take careful note of the geometric shapes and patterns present in the various components of the house.

The garden and lawns of a traditional timber house are a vital component, offering cool shade, colour and delight. They are worth careful attention.

GARDENS AND OUTBUILDINGS

A garden is one of the most important elements in the environment of a tropical house and is therefore worth careful attention. It offers delight, cool shade, enjoyment and colour. The old garden where trees and shrubs have taken a long time to grow requires special consideration, so avoid indiscriminate tearing out of plants which may well have become an important part of the ecology of the area. Plan carefully and take into account any possible effect which changes may have on the local wild life.

The back garden, especially, can be full of interesting and useful trees such as the mango, loquat or citrus. The owner may have some pet hate of over-colourful exotic trees, annuals, or trees that constantly drop their leaves. There are many ways to solve such problems. For instance heavy planting with green everlasting trees and shrubs can tone down colourful varieties and

can actually enhance their good features. Similarly flowers, whether annuals or perennials, can look delightful when scattered about in a 'wild' garden or under trees with an open foliage.

Outbuildings may refer to anything from tool sheds, tea-houses, pavilions and garages to fountains, drives and footpaths. Although paths and drives require a good hard-wearing surface, large expansive concrete areas are difficult to demolish and remove. Less fixed pavings like brick, block or flagstones can be more easily altered. Such pavings can be effectively laid on a bed of sand which allows the rain to seep through to the soil below. Another good method lies in spreading finely crushed stone on a levelled ground.

The best way to select appropriate materials for a new fence or a garden wall is to study carefully the house itself. A timber house, for instance, is likely to sit more comfortably with a timber fence. Likewise the style of the house can be a guide to the design of a fence. In most cases it is better to

follow the design of the existing fence on the property and thus ensure the continuity of theme and character established by the original builders.

Garages and carports can pose a problem but are easier to deal with if the house has been raised on high timber stumps. They can be locked up with swinging gates made from timber laths that have been removed from the spaces between stumps to provide direct access to the car. Use of the underneath area can also be extended to provide a workshop, laundry or a playroom for children. These look better if set well back from the perimeter wall and are relatively unobtrusive. Low-level houses can be extended horizontally by discreetly building a lean-to in the same materials as the house itself, using light timber laths and corrugated metal sheet roofs which effectively let in filtered light and air but remain secure and somewhat well hidden. It is possible to see many good examples of such structures attached to and harmonising happily with old tropical houses in northern Australia.

RESTORATION & RENOVATION

INTERIORS

Generally rooms of old tropical houses are easy to alter as their walls are normally single-skinned and framing is fairly straightforward. Doors and windows can be easily inserted, closed verandahs can be re-opened and whole wall panels can be removed by replacing them with simple timber beams to support the light roof.

A major feature of tropical living is the close relationship which exists between indoors and outdoors. For instance, the doors of most rooms normally open directly on to the surrounding verandah. It is important to bear this relationship in mind when alterations and extensions are planned. An attractive outdoor barbecue terrace is less functional if it is accessible only from the front door or if it is a long way from the kitchen.

As in exterior surfaces, the first essential step is to make a routine check for termites and rot. Freshly painted or wallpapered surfaces often hide stains from leaky roofs, plumbing leaks, termite damage and rot. Tapping a surface can often indicate possible defects. A hollow dull thud means problems which should be re-checked by poking a pocket knife or even car keys into the area.

If it is necessary to replace timber, then a browse through timber yards is likely to reveal the difficulties in obtaining 12 inch horizontal boards often used in old structures. Other smaller sizes, such as vertical v-jointed boarding (standard 4 x ¾ inch), are easier to find and perform equally well.

Many functional problems of old timber houses are caused by movement and settlements. There are gaps in skirtings and, owing to irregular alignments, doors and windows become fixed and are difficult to open. Doors can be planed back to fit but the problems may surface again when the house is levelled again at a later stage.

Doors and windows are fairly expensive to replace. Demolition sales and second-hand building materials yards are often a good source for picking up matching items. French doors are expensive but are usually well worth the high cost, as they admirably lend themselves to linking the indoors with the outdoors. Some manufacturers are now willing to make special doors and windows with traditional silky oak frames to meet specific requirements.

It is equally important to look out for good quality old locks, knobs and latches as they harmonise better with old traditional tropical buildings than new designs.

V-jointed section walls in traditional houses are structural elements but, with proper care, holes can still be cut for openings. An architect or builder can advise as to what is feasible. The aim should be to cut with a trim that matches the existing jambs and heads. Some demolition yards occasionally sell old decorative archways, (ideal as room dividers).

Ceilings

Most larger tropical houses have high ceilings which are indeed a great asset. They provide a great sense of space, light, air and ventilation. Stains indicate possible leaks, and cornices with gaps and loose fit to the corners could mean the house has settled irregularly. Ceiling frames of some early houses are lined with stamped metal which is highly decorative and is therefore worth careful restoration.

It is also necessary to periodically examine the space above the ceilings which is accessible through a manhole. Roof ventilation is essential. Vents in some roofs are large and form an important feature of the roof-top. Others may require additional fixtures to ensure adequate circulation. Other items frequently found in the roof include possums, carpet snakes, birds nests, all of which must be eradicated with the help of pest control experts. Bird-proof nets can be installed under the eaves.

As mentioned elsewhere, the roof is a major source of heat gain in a house. It is important to provide some form of insulation above the ceiling to keep the house cool during summer and warm during winter. Also, check the flues and chimneys of heaters and fireplaces. Brick chimneys are safe but heat-proof and fire-proof lining must be provided for bare fibro and metal flues to accord with the local building codes and requirements of insurance companies. And, finally, a minimum height of nine feet (2.75 metres) is required for safe installation of a ceiling fan.

Kitchens

Kitchens can be relocated — as the old timber houses allow easy penetration of the floor to fit new services. It is fairly easy to build a new kitchen in a better location while the old one is still in service. If major additions are envisaged, then it might be useful to consider the kitchen part of that breezy open living space that may project from the back verandah. Modern fittings will not look out of place. It is often more convenient to install new fittings than to recondition existing fittings.

If the kitchen is in an original condition, it may have an old cast iron enamelled sink, an early 'Kooka' gas stove, a dresser, a fridge that frosts up all the time, a table and a couple of chairs. To renovate kitchens it is best to consider how the room or galley will be used. Will the table be used for eating? If so, adequate room will have to be provided. The main object is to plan the kitchen to function simply and efficiently. Provide adequate bench space. Ventilation is very important in the kitchen as the stove is likely to give off heat, steam, and, sometimes, smoke. Good light for preparation and a pleasant view outdoors while doing the dishes is desirable. Avoid having a kitchen facing westwards, as it will be unbearable in summer. Storage and bench space are the most difficult things to design. Open storage shelves are the most accessible and the best ventilated. If an 'appearance' of total neatness is desired, a pantry with a door might be the solution. Pantries must be well ventilated and cool. Shallow shelves running up the wall are much better than deep cupboards under the benches.

Floor coverings for kitchens must be hard-wearing and easy to clean. There are many alternatives: cork tiles, vinyl tiles, sheet vinyl, ceramic and quarry tiles.

Bathrooms

Older bathrooms can be a problem, especially if they have an instantaneous gas heater for the shower and bath and not for the basin. A further difficulty arises if, in order to replace the back-yard closet, the WC has been squeezed into an already tight space upstairs. For a buyer, it is important to note whether firstly, the bathroom can be used right away and, secondly, whether a new hot water system has to be installed. It is also necessary to test all taps and to check that the WC flushes efficiently. Poor pressure can indicate rusty pipes.

If there is already a toilet, bath/shower and basin installed, and the position is satisfactory but the items either don't work or look inappropriate, then refitting and a face-lift is required. New fittings and tile surfaces can be installed at reasonable prices.

Toilets and cisterns are not expensive to replace. The operation is likely to be more expensive, however, if the positions are drastically changed. Fortunately, the elevated tropical house is ideal for swapping room functions at a moderate cost. Pipes can be suspended under the floor before they enter the ground. The real expense lies in digging up, repairing and laying new sewage pipes. The single-skin internal walls do not allow the plumbing in the walls to be hidden from view. Pipes will have to pass through the floor and will therefore be exposed. Neatly fitted plumbing is not unattractive.

Timber Pests

In tropical areas, the worst enemy of timber structures are pests such as white ants and borers.

White ants usually nest in contact with the ground, sometimes under and at other times above ground around a stump. They need moisture to survive, so, if the stump is damp, it can often support a colony of white ants free from the ground. White ants are unable to survive solely within the damp and dark protection of their mud house; so they build mud-covered runways to reach favoured timber above the ground and start climbing up and into the house proper. They can be found over brickwork, concrete, and even over ant-resistant poison-impregnated timber.

This is one of the many explanations offered as to why, in some areas, the traditional tropical house was built on elevated stumps as this then enabled its owners to inspect early signs of white ant infestation. Usually there is little one can do except to replace affected timber with timber that is naturally resistant, or else ensure that all stumps have been topped with ant-caps with the edges curled downwards to make it difficult for ants to climb upwards. However, experience indicates that all such measures are not entirely infallible. Carelessly placed nails and rusted ant-caps provide easy access to these pests enabling them to climb through the house unnoticed.

If an ant nest or runway is discovered, then the best advice can be obtained from the State Department of Forestry or from the officers of the Commonwealth Experimental Building Station at North Ryde near Sydney. Appropriate advice is essential because poisons are extremely dangerous and are not always very effective.

Borers are just as destructive and potentially dangerous as the white ants. One can easily fall through a heavily infested timber floor. Borers do not nest; they are beetles which lay eggs in timber. The eggs hatch and the larvae tunnel through the timber until the chrysalis is formed just under the surface, allowing the beetle to escape and thus repeat the cycle.

Most of the problems are presented by only three species of borers, namely the Lyctus, the West Indian Drywood, and the Anobium. Lyctus attacks seasoned and partly seasoned timber, bores 1/32 to 1/16 inch diameter round holes and galleries along the grain of the timber which are tightly packed by fine, smooth and floury dust.

The West Indian Drywood borer attacks seasoned timber, mainly pine and old furniture. It is more dangerous and is known to destroy homes. It leaves small pellets in a heap which are hard and have a sandy feel about them. The Anobium is also known as the Furniture or Hoop-pine borer and is only found in seasoned timber several years old. It bores approximately 1/16 inch diameter holes and galleries along the grain and generates abundant loose dust which is gritty like fine table salt.

In all cases of heavily borer-infested timber, it is best to replace it rather than treat it. Slight borer attack requires saturation of the affected areas with an approved poison. The advice of the Forestry Department officials is again helpful here. Re-infestation can be prevented by sealing the surface with paint or any one of the clear finishes with a heavy zinc base.

There are other borers which attack green timber only but, once the timber is properly seasoned, re-infestation is unlikely to occur again. Such borers are known as the 'pinhole' variety as they leave tiny holes which show up after the cleaning or sanding of old floor boards. These borers should not cause concern.

Building components of traditional houses can often be bought cheaply at demolition sales.

Long established deciduous trees provide shade during the hot summer months yet allow the winter sun to penetrate living areas.

A WORD ON PAINTING

Apart from improving the appearance of a building, painting adds years to the life of such materials as exposed timber and metal. Hardware and paint shops offer a large range of paints. However it is important to choose the most appropriate paint for a specific job. Paints have an enamel, vinyl or acrylic base and can provide a flat, semi-gloss to a gloss finish. Enamels and acrylic are most popular as they are easiest to apply; but special care is required when choosing paints for bathrooms and kitchens, because both these areas harbour moisture and grime and therefore require constant maintenance and upkeep. It is important not to buy cheap varieties of paint and brushes and it is equally important to strictly follow the manufacturer's instructions, particularly taking special care to prepare the surface before the actual painting.

There are special paints available for metal roofs which are rust-proof and give a good clean appearance to what is one of the most dominating features of a house. It is advisable to avoid dark heat-absorbing colours in tropical climates and choose instead white or light colours which are the most effective in reflecting the heat from the sun.

The same principles apply for selecting paints for the interior of the house. Interiors offer a greater scope for experimenting with colours which will harmonise with furnishings and the orientation and location of windows and doors.

There are many ways to finish timber floors which are not likely to be carpeted or covered with tiles. Often floors of old houses have been constructed with excellent timbers which reveal their real qualities after cleaning and sanding. Such floors can be effectively finished with a coat or two of polyurethane liquids and stains.

SOME LEGAL MATTERS

It is important to remember that all major alterations, renovations and additions require the approval of the local council who normally require reasonably comprehensive documents explaining what is intended. Here an architect or a design draughtsman can assist. It is advisable to engage a builder who is registered under the House Builders Registration Act who can take legal responsibility for ensuring a high standard of workmanship.

The best way to select appropriate materials for restoration and renovation is to study the house itself to ensure continuity of the theme and character established by its original owners.

Right *This freshly painted house displays the rewards of constant maintenance.*

FURTHER READING

BAGLIN, D. and MOFFITT, P. *The Australian Verandah*. Paul Hamlyn, Sydney, 1978.

BELL, P. 'Houses in North Queensland Mining Towns, 1864 - 1914' *Readings in North Queensland Mining History*, Vol. 1. Edited by K.H. Kennedy, History Department, James Cook University, 1980.
Vernacular Domestic Architecture in North Queensland Mining Towns: Interim Report to the Australian Heritage Commission. History Department, James Cook University, June, 1979.

BLAINEY, G. *The Tyranny of Distance*. Sun, Melbourne, 1966.

BOLTON, G.C. *A Thousand Miles Away*. Jacaranda Press in association with A.N.U. Press, 1963.

BOYD, R. *Australia's Home*. Penguin, Ringwood, 1968.

CILENTO, R.W. *The White Man in the Tropics*. Department of Health Services Publication No. 7, Government Printer, Melbourne, 1927.

COX, P. and FREELAND, J. *Rude Timber Buildings in Australia*. Thames and Hudson, London, 1969.

COX, P. and STACEY, W. *Historic Towns of Australia*. Lansdowne Press, Sydney, 1973.
The Australian Homestead. Lansdowne Press, Sydney, 1972.

FRAZER SMITH, J. *White Pillars - The Architecture of the South*. Brainhall Press, New York, MCMXLI.

FREELAND, J.M. *Architecture in Australia*. Pelican, Ringwood, 1972.

GIVONI, B. *Man, Climate and Architecture*. Elsevier, Amsterdam, 1969.

GRAY, B. *Reminiscences of India and North Queensland*. Constable, London, 1913.

HOGAN, J. *Historic Homes of Brisbane*. National Trust of Queensland, Brisbane, 1979.

HOLMES, M.J. *Australia's Open North*. Angus and Robertson, Sydney, 1963.

KENNEDY, K.H. ed. *Readings in North Queensland Mining History*. James Cook University, Townsville, 1980.

KING, A.D. 'The Bungalow: the Development and Diffusion of a House Type'. *Architectural Association Quarterly*, Vol. 5, No. 3, London, 1973.
Colonial Urban Development. Routledge and Kegan Paul, London, 1976.

LUCAS, C. *Conservation and Restoration of Buildings — Philosophy and Approach*. Australian Council of National Trusts, Sydney, 1978.
Conservation and Restoration of Buildings — Preservation of Roofs. Australian Council of National Trusts, Sydney, 1979.

MARSDEN, B.S. 'A Century of Building Materials in Queensland and Brisbane, 1861-1961'. *Australian Geographer* x(2), 1966.

MORRISON, H. *Early American Architecture*. Oxford University Press, New York, 1952.

NATIONAL TRUST OF QUEENSLAND, *A study of the Tent House in Fourth Avenue, Mount Isa*. 1977.
A Walk and Drive of Cairns. 1978.
A Walk and Drive of Maryborough. 1979.
A Walk and Drive of Rockhampton. 1977.
A Walk and Drive of Rockhampton together with a Drive of nearby Mount Morgan. 1981.
A Walk Through Brisbane: Ann Street, Wickham Terrace. 1976, 1979.
A Walk Through Brisbane: South East City. 1976.
A Walk Through Brisbane: North East City. 1977.
Ipswich: A Townscape Study. 1977.
Listings Register, Brisbane. 1977.

NILSSON, S. *European Architecture in India 1750-1850*. Faber & Faber, London, 1968.

PAYNTER, J. 'The Australian Verandah'. *Architecture in Australia*. Official Journal of R.A.I.A., Sydney, Vol. 54, No. 52, June, 1965.

POWER, R. *Historic Houses of Australia*. Cassell, Melbourne, 1974.

PRICE, A.G. 'White Settlers in the Tropics'. *American Geog. Soc. Special Publication* No. 23, 1939.

RAPOPORT, A. *House Form and Culture*. Prentice Hall, Englewood Cliffs, New Jersey, 1969.

RODERICK, D. 'House at the corner of Hodgkinson and High Streets'. *Historic Houses of Australia*. Cassell, Melbourne, 1974.

SAINI, B. *Architecture in Tropical Australia*. Melbourne University Press, Melbourne, 1970.
Building in Hot, Dry Climates. John Wiley & Sons, London, 1980.

SHAND, R.I. 'Report' on Investigation into the Design of Houses for the Commonwealth Railways'. *Architecture in Australia*, Official Journal of R.A.I.A., Vol. 52, No. 1, March, 1963.

SUMNER, R. *Settlers and Habitat*. Monograph Series No. 6, Department of Geography, James Cook University, 1974.

WATSON, D. *Dating Your House*. The National Trust of Queensland, Brisbane, 1978.

WHITE, U.N.K., JOPSON, K., NEWELL, P. and ROBERTS, A. *Queensland Sketchbook*. Rigby, Sydney, 1976.

GLOSSARY

Acroteria An ornamental pedestal designed to support sculptural forms.

Ant-Cap A special cap used on top of wooden stumps to prevent white ants from climbing upwards and damaging the house.

Architrave A term commonly applied to the moulded frame surrounding a door, a window or arch.

Art Nouveau A movement away from imitation of the past; characterised by undulating curves, particularly in the form of flowing hair, flames and flower stalks. It flourished at the beginning of the twentieth century and took its name from an art shop in Paris. The movement spread internationally and was reflected in all the arts.

Baluster (a) A post supporting the handrail of a staircase. (b) Decorative pillar supporting a railing.

Balustrade A series of balusters resting on a base and supporting a continuous horizontal railing or coping.

Bearer Any horizontal beam, joist or member which supports a load.

Bressummer Usually a large beam, sometimes elaborately carved, which extends across a wide opening such as a fireplace or screen. Also the main horizontal rail in a timber frame house.

Bungalow Originally, a single-storey, lightly built house with verandah used by the British in India. The word is derived from the Hindi 'Bangla', meaning 'belonging to Bengal'.

Chamferboard A form of cladding nailed flush to the studs and overlapped by means of rebates or chamfers on each board. It is similar to 'ship-lap' or 'lapped boards'.

Classical Style Referring to the architecture of ancient Greece and Rome, on which the Italian Renaissance and later styles (such at the Baroque and the classical revival) were based.

Entablature In classical architecture, the superstructure above the column, comprising the architrave, frieze and cornice.

Facade The front or face of a building.

Fascia A plain horizontal board which masks the ends of rafters under the eaves.

Finial Carved or moulded ornament crowning a gable, pinnacle or spire.

French Empire Style A term applied mainly to a style of interior decoration and furniture which began in Paris after the French Revolution and subsequently spread through Europe. It corresponds to the Regency style in England.

French Windows Windows reaching to ground level and opening like a pair of doors.

Gable The upper triangular portion of an external wall beneath a pitched roof.

Gablet A small roof gable.

Georgian Style A mode of architecture prevalent in England during the reigns of the first four King Georges. Its basis was Italian, derived from styles introduced by Andrea Palladio. Some of the finest examples of early colonial architecture in Australia are Georgian.

Gothic Architecture The dominant style in Europe from the middle of the twelfth century to the end of the fifteenth century. Its features were the ribbed vault, the pointed arch and use of stained glass windows.

Gothic Revival Also called Neo-Gothic. An architectural style which originated during the eighteenth century and flourished especially in the nineteenth century. It aimed at reviving the spirit and forms of Gothic architecture.

Greek Revival Style The renewal of interest in the architecture of Hellenic Greece, which took place in the late eighteenth and early nineteenth centuries.

High Stump A two to three metres high round trinker column used to elevate the house above ground.

Joist A timber support or a series of parallel beams for a floor or ceiling, which in turn are supported by large beams or girders.

Lath A thin narrow strip of wood used as a base for the walls and ceiling. Originally a sawn strip of wood used as a foundation for plaster. The term is also used for other materials which serve as a foundation for plaster work, for example metal lathing.

Lintel A horizontal member supported at each end and carrying a weight — as across a flat-headed door or window.

Neo-classicism A term used for the eighteenth century revival of classical architecture which arose as a reaction against excesses of Rococo. In England it was popularised by the Adam brothers and James Wyatt.

Pediment (a) A decorative feature finishing the gable end of a classical building. (b) A decoration of geometric shape over a wall opening, such as a doorway or window.

Regency Style The neo-classic architectural style which became popular in England during the period 1811-20 when the Prince Regent (later King George IV) was administering affairs of state on behalf of his ailing father, George III. It was an elegant and colourful style, making extensive use of painted stucco and refinement of classical forms.

Renaissance Architecture A style originating in Florence, Italy, during the early fifteenth century, whence it spread to most of Italy and began replacing the Gothic style of the middle ages throughout Europe. It revived classical forms and ornament, such as the column and round arch, the tunnel vault and dome. Renaissance is a French word meaning 'rebirth' and is used to describe the transition period from the mediaeval to the modern world.

Shingles Thin wooden slips used as roofing tiles. In early Australia, shingles split from native timbers were employed extensively.

Skirting A moulded wooden member along the base of an internal wall, covering the joint between wall and floor.

Stucco A kind of plaster rendering applied to an external wall, suitable for modelling and moulding.

Terracotta A baked form of fine brick earth.

Tudor Architecture A late form of Gothic which flourished in England during the reigns of the Tudors. It was characterised by depressed, four-centred arches, shal-

GLOSSARY

low mouldings and a predominance of panelling on the walls.

Verandah Of Eastern name and origin, a light external gallery with sloping roof, awning-like, supported on slender pillars and frequently partly enclosed with lattice work.

Victorian Architecture The Revival and Eclectic architecture of nineteenth century Britain which took its name from the reign of Queen Victoria (1837-1901).

Villa Originally the residence of a Roman landowner, the term has long been applied to country and suburban houses standing alone.

INDEX

Text references appear in bold type.

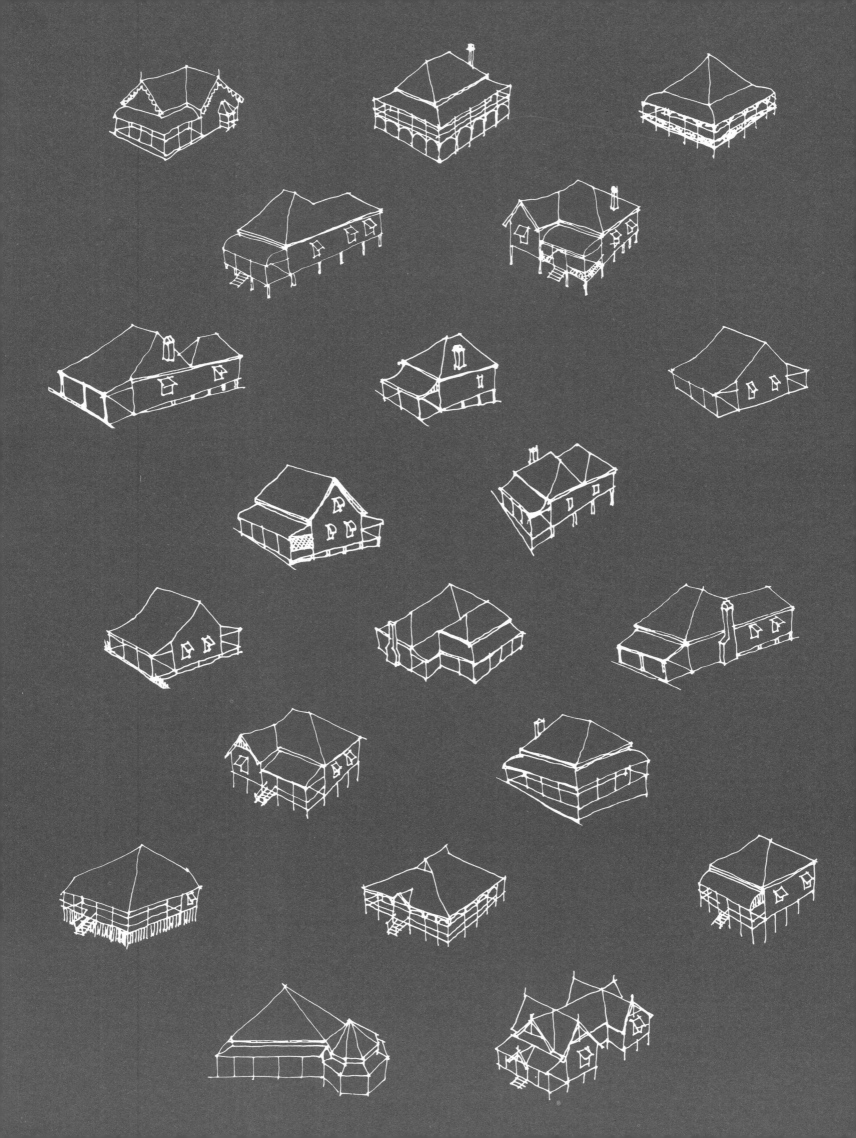